The Red Report

When Banks Don't Compete

– The Case Of The Mortgage Calculator –

By Leon L. Morris

Telephone (678) 388-7823

Table of Contents

Part Four: Study Results

Part Five: Implications & Applications

Part Six: Conclusion

Appendix A: Individual MSA Results by State (Continued)

Abstract

This study tested the accuracy of Rent v. Buy (RvB) financial calculators made available online by state and federally chartered banks with a 1% or greater market share of FDIC insured bank deposits in the largest metropolitan-area in each of the 50 states. Three model client scenarios, Section 5 of the Federal Trade Commission Act and the Herfendahl-Hirschman Index of market concentration served as benchmarks. All RvB calculators tested proved defective, overstating the tax benefits of the mortgage interest deduction by more than 250% while failing to disclose currently available tax benefits and/or allowing for an all cash purchase option, thus distorting housing and mortgage affordability and suitability while perpetuating a cultural and institutionalized financial bias and a lack of objective financial or mortgage advice.

Executive Summary

This report presents the findings of testing performed on mortgage calculators provided on and through websites of hundreds of banks from all fifty states with the largest market share of deposits in the largest metropolitan areas. Calculators that purport to calculate the tax savings in a standard rent versus buy decision were tested for accuracy using a Model Client Scenario. Although the bank websites usually posted a disclaimer regarding the accuracy of the calculators, due to a bank's name and reputation a consumer may not discount the results entirely. Therefore, as a result of using these calculators, a consumer's expectations about increased tax savings due to homeownership could influence a consumer's view of housing affordability and suitability. The report identifies all bank websites reviewed and details the findings for each.

During the study, it was found that many of the banks touted the conversion rate of capturing prospects and converting them into 'interested and motivated' mortgage applicants as a result of using these calculators. Therefore, unless it is disclosed to consumers that these calculators are mortgage-marketing tools, consumers may view the provision of mortgage calculators as a free and objective consumer service provided by the banks. Consequently, based on a belief that these calculators are reliable, a faulty mortgage calculator may play a role in consumers deciding to buy homes that, but for the inaccurate results of these calculators, they may have realized that they could not afford. To the extent that consumers initiate mortgage transactions due to these inaccurate mortgage calculators, it may fall under the Federal Trade Commission's definition of an unfair and/or deceptive act and/or practice. Additionally, to the extent that faulty mortgage calculators distort a consumer's view of housing affordability and suitability, these calculators could impact mortgage defaults, foreclosures and property tax collections.

The Herfindahl-Hirschman Index (HHI) of market concentration was used as an indicator of market concentration and presumed market power. Institutions that have market power have the ability to engage in anti-competitive behavior, which among other things discourages competition, innovation and leads to inefficient markets. The HHI is the same tool the Federal Trade Commission (FTC) and Department of Justice (DOJ) use to interpret market data relative to market concentration. Transactions that raise the HHI by more than 100 points in moderately concentrated markets or more than 50 points in highly concentrated markets presumptively raises "significant competitive concerns" under the Horizontal Merger Guidelines issued by the DOJ and the FTC. A merger is presumed "likely to create or enhance market power or facilitate its exercise" if the HHI increases by more than 100 points. The average and median post HHI, in this study, for all Metropolitan Statistical Areas rose by 3096 and 3015 points respectively, 30 times the guideline.

In employing the HHI, this study treats a faulty mortgage calculator as the product being sold/or being made available by banks. However, the study recognizes that the banks may or may not be the creator of the faulty calculator, but the faulty calculator is accessible on or through bank websites. In order to get an idea of what the market looked like in each MSA, as it relates to the calculations in question, only institutions that made a faulty calculator available on or through their websites were treated as if they merged.

The report confirms that predatory lending practices are not limited to the sub-prime mortgage market as is generally believed. The Report also implies that adults consistently demonstrate difficulty understanding basic financial concepts and have difficulty distinguishing the difference between financial-education and marketing communications. Testing of mortgage calculators promoted by or linked from entities such as Ginnie Mae, the Department of Housing and Urban Development, Freddie Mac and the President's Financial Literacy and Education Commission (Links to Ginnie Mae Calculator) also uncovered surprising results that demonstrate an overwhelming need for mortgage advisors who have a fiduciary responsibility to the consumer. Some of these entities are quasi-governmental agencies, and the Financial Literacy and Education Commission was created to promote financial literacy; however, the mortgage calculators they provided or promoted were found to be unreliable.

The widespread nature of web access and the diverse demographic characteristics of those using one of these calculators would make it difficult to determine the full extent of any harm caused by their use and any such findings are beyond the scope of this study.

The report concludes that defective mortgage calculators overstate the tax benefits of the mortgage interest deduction, and thereby perpetuate a nationwide financial bias in that regard. Missing in all homeownership information reviewed is acknowledgement that homeownership has a quantifiable benefits and values even in the absence of a mortgage that is at least six (6) times greater than the mortgage interest deduction. Information regarding this seldom documented benefit is put forth in this report and examples are provided as to how it should be quantified. The report demonstrates why these benefits and values are essential in making informed homeownership decisions.

PART ONE: **Introduction**

Predatory Lending Defined

In 2000, the HUD-Treasury National Predatory Lending Task Force issued a report about predatory lending and predatory lending practices that was well received as it focused on predatory lenders and predatory lending practices in the subprime mortgage market. The report defined predatory lending whether undertaken by creditors, brokers, or home improvement contractors as engaging in deception or fraud, manipulating the borrower through aggressive sales tactics, or taking unfair advantage of a borrower's lack of understanding about loan terms and that these practices are often combined with loan terms that, alone or in combination, are abusive or make the borrowers more vulnerable to abusive practices.

The HUD-Treasury report held that predatory lending was generally a subprime problem involving borrowers who for a variety of reasons have limited access to the extensively regulated mainstream financial sector and where a majority of the mortgage loans are debt consolidation loans as opposed to money purchase loans. Research conducted by HUD in connection with the National Predatory Lending Task Force found that even after controlling for neighborhood income (although without controlling for credit history or risk), subprime lending (and predatory practices) tends to be concentrated in low-income and predominantly African-American communities. The report concluded that while predatory lending could occur in the prime mortgage market, because banks, thrifts and credit unions are subjected to such extensive federal and state oversight and supervision, unlike many of their subprime counter parts, it was ordinarily deterred because there was greater competition among lenders, greater homogeneity in loan terms and greater financial information among borrowers who live in predominantly white communities.

Objective

This report acknowledges that homeownership is widely promoted and highly sought after as the American dream and focuses on one of the many entrances to that dream in the prime mortgage market, online access to the self-help area made available on or through the websites of banks and thrifts where prime consumers (of all types) have their money on deposit and where they can conveniently begin to address the question of whether buying or renting a home is in their best interest. This report challenges conventional wisdom not only by focusing on the acquisition aspect of the American dream by Americans generally (including those in the predominant community) at the very beginning of the process, but also by recognizing two other previously under emphasized acknowledgements made in the HUD-Treasury Report: (1) that "predatory lending practices can occur at any stage of the loan process..." and (2) that predatory lending practices can "be undertaken, or at least facilitated, by any of the many participants in a particular transaction"[i] and that includes those traditionally thought of as being subjected to extensive regulation at the state and federal level, such as banks, thrifts and credit unions.

A Calculator In The Public Domain

The American Heritage Dictionary defines calculator as follows: "1. One that calculates, as: a. An electronic or mechanical device for the performance of mathematical computations. b. A person who operates such a machine or otherwise makes calculations. 2. A set of mathematical tables used to aid in calculating."

This research is approached from the perspective that most adults view a calculator as a tool. The expectation being that the tool will help accomplish the task the tool was designed to perform. There is an expectation that a calculator designed to answer a question or series of questions will answer the question correctly when used as instructed.

PART TWO: **Study Methods and Populations**

Secondary Data:

Given the dual banking system in the U.S., a conscientious effort was made to avoid selection bias relative to where a bank, thrift or credit union was domiciled (in state or out of state), and whether or not the bank, thrift or credit union was under the primary supervision of the Office of the Comptroller of the Currency[ii], the Federal Reserve Board, the Office of Thrift Supervision[iii], or a state regulator. In researching both the availability and suitability of secondary data relative to bank lists, the data available from the FDIC from the insured institutions annual Summary of Deposit (SOD) survey was a natural fit (given available resources). The financial institutions listed in the SOD includes banks and thrifts that are federally or state chartered with one common denominator, they are all FDIC insured institutions.

The FDIC insured institutions annual SOD survey was the primary source of secondary data used in this report. The FDIC requires every federally insured depository institution to file an annual report detailing the deposit balances or volumes at each of its banking offices or branches. The FDIC collects deposit balances for commercial and savings banks as of June 30 of each year, and the Office of Thrift Supervision (OTS) collects the same data for savings institutions. The reports are a required annual filing and the results are usually released by the end of October each year. The SOD is the sole source of OTS branch information derived from the annually collected Branch Office Survey. The SOD contains deposit data for more than 80,000 branches/offices of FDIC-insured institutions. The June 30, 2006, data is used in this study. The June 30, 2006, data was the latest annual data available as of October 1, 2007. The law and FTC regulations also served as a secondary data source for prescriptive, descriptive and prohibited practices.

Institutional Subjects:

The sample for this study was obtained by making use of the SOD data, which covered all FDIC insured institutions. All FDIC insured institutions were then separated geographically into fifty groups based upon depository data by state and then by depository data in the largest Metropolitan Statistical Area (MSA) in each state. The states of New York and New Jersey shared the same metropolitan statistical area. To avoid favoring one state over the other no adjustment was made by seeking a second or the next smaller MSA for either state.

The SOD data identified all FDIC insured financial institutions in each MSA for a total of 3,535 (New York data included). Each MSA was treated as an independent sample for purposes of identifying individual institutional and aggregate market share data for or in each MSA. Websites were reviewed for all financial institutions clustered within each MSA that have 1% or greater market share and all simple and complex (Rent v. Buy (RvB) or Save in Tax (SiTx)) mortgage calculators that were available on or through those websites were examined.

The One Percenters (1%ers):

For the sake of brevity, in this report, those institutions that have a 1% or greater market share individually and collectively are referred to as the "one percenters." The one percenters are identified in one of three ways: (1) as a one percenter with no complex mortgage calculator (NCMC), (2) as a one percenter with perfectly or properly functioning complex mortgage calculator (PCMC) and (3) a one percenter with a deficient complex mortgage calculator (DCMC). The aggregate number of one percenters from all MSAs is 674 and the range is a low of 3 to a high of 23. The average number of FDIC insured institutions in a MSA among one percenters is 13.50. The median is 14.

Herfendahl-Hirschmann Index (HHI) :

In an effort to understand, measure, communicate and summarize any DCMC data and the anti-competitive nature (potential antitrust implications) of DCMCs in each of the MSA, this research employed the same tool the FTC and Department of Justice (DOJ) use to interpret market data relative to market concentration, the Herfindahl-Hirschman Index (HHI) of market concentration. Transactions that raise the HHI by more than 100 points in moderately concentrated markets or by more than 50 points in highly concentrated markets presumptively raise "significant competitive concerns" under the Horizontal Merger Guidelines issued by the DOJ and the FTC. A merger is presumed "likely to create or enhance market power or facilitate its exercise" if the HHI increases by more than 100 points.

Because the Herfindahl-Hirschman Index (HHI) of market concentration is based upon the market share of each financial institution in the market, each institution in each MSA is included in calculating the HHI as it exists in the market and also on a Pro Forma basis. The Pro Forma data is used to represent the market share concentration of those banks that are part of the one percenters with a DCMC. Those with a DCMC are treated as if they had merged and the HHI is then recalculated on a post-merger Pro Forma basis. The indexes are then compared. The number of financial institutions (pre-merger) in a MSA ranges from a low of five (5) to a high of three-hundred and five (305), and the average MSA has 71 financial institutions pre-merger. The median number of financial institutions in a MSA is 45. The Please note, the actual HHI point difference between the 1%ers in an MSA and the MSA HHI on average is less than 14 points overall for all MSAs and the range is .0001 - 13.7041.

PART THREE: **Study Procedure**

Primary Data Collection:

An Excel ® spreadsheet was used to develop a data collection form for recording what was observed on the websites of the one percenters. The data collection form included the state, MSA, the financial institution's name, FDIC certificate number, primary website address, market share, provision of a Rent versus Buy or a Save in Tax (SiTx) complex mortgage calculator on the website and notation of whether or not the calculator(s) performed correctly. Other column headings on the data collection form included notations for whether or not the mortgage calculator web-page displayed or showed the following: disclaimer regarding mortgage calculator, bank name on the web-page, home equity loans to consolidate debt-taxes, mortgage payment calculated, tax savings calculated, tax deduction mentioned, and other/tax exemptions mentioned. Supporting documentation includes a letter size printed copy of each website visited, and if the website had a complex mortgage calculator page, a copy of the page was saved in a portable document format.

The only information found on the use of mortgage calculators by industry came from software vendors and information made available from trade association meetings.

Apparatus:

All data calculations performed during this research were made on a windows based personal computer using Microsoft Excel ® spreadsheet software. The personal computer had a modem and Internet access via a high-speed digital subscriber line from AT&T. Portable document format printer software was used to print screen shots of all websites visited and the calculations made by Rent v Buy (RvB) or Save in Taxes (SiTx) complex mortgage calculators. The secondary data source for market share information was the Federal Deposit Insurance Corporation (FDIC) insured institutions annual Summary of Deposit (SOD) survey.

Regulations, guidelines, prohibitations and advisory letters issued by four federal regulatory authorities (FTC, OCC, FDIC and FRB) against unfair or deceptive acts or practices are used in describing the legal standard these regulators use in determining whether an act or practice is unfair or deceptive. Tax tools used included several IRS publications: #527 (Residential Rental Property), #530 (Tax Information for First-Time Homeowners), #936 (Home Mortgage Interest Deduction), tax tables for 2006, and instructions for Schedule A and E on Form 1040. The FTC guidelines on horizontal mergers are another tool used to analyze market concentration. Horizontal mergers occur when banks competing in the same market merge or join together. For purposes of this study, those who make RvB calculators available on or through their websites are treated as having merged on a pro forma basis. The Herfindahl-Hirschman Index (HHI) of market concentration was used. (The HHI is calculated by squaring the market share of each firm competing in the market and then summing the resulting numbers).

Like the websites, all the critical tools used in this study are readily available online to the general public. Websites maybe identified.

Calculators Reviewed:

An analysis of the following type calculators was undertaken. Examples of language that appears on the web pages are shown below:

(A) Simple Mortgage Calculator:

May be listed as “mortgage” or “loan” calculator or by a heading such as “How Much Is Your Monthly Payment?” These calculators help an individual determine the amount of a monthly payment given a stated loan amount, interest rate and period. The calculators can also be used to explore the outcome of changes to a loan balance, mortgage term, interest rate or payment amount. The calculators can be used in home buying or refinancing situations.

(B) Complex Mortgage Calculator (CMC):

For example, the Bank of America website says, “Crunch the numbers then start your loan[iv].” Then after clicking on “Am I better off renting or owning?” a new page appears and among the things that appear at the top of the page after the **Bank of America** logo in a bolded 12-point red print font is “**Calculator: Am I Better off renting or owning?**” At the bottom of the page, after the inputs, is **“important note about this calculator:”** and written in what appears to be a 7 point-print font is the following: “The calculators are provided by one or more third party providers. The figures entered on the input page of this calculator are for hypothetical purposes only. You should enter figures that are appropriate to your individual situation. The results provided by this calculator are also intended for illustrative purposes only and accuracy is not guaranteed. Bank of America and its affiliates are not tax or legal advisers. This calculator is not intended to offer any tax, legal, financial or investment advice and does not assure the availability of or your eligibility for any specific product offered by Bank of America, its affiliates or any other institution, nor does this calculator predict or guarantee the actual results of any investment products. The terms and conditions of products offered by institutions will differ and may affect the results of the calculator. Please consult with qualified professionals to discuss your situation.” [v]

(1) Rent versus Buy Calculator (RvB):

“This calculator allows you to compare renting versus buying by entering how much you want to spend a month and how much down you would put into your house.”[vi] “Buying a home entails more costs than what’s reflected in your monthly payment. For some, buying is the right answer, but for others, renting is the way to go. Considering all of the costs and tax implications will lead to a better decision.”[vii] A third example: “Should you rent or should you buy your home? It takes more than looking at your mortgage payment to answer this question. This calculator helps you weed through the fees, taxes, and monthly payments to help you make a good financial decision. Click the "View Report" button for a detailed look at the results.”[viii]

(2) Save In Tax Calculator (SiTx):

The calculator heading may read “How Much Can I Save In Taxes?” “This calculator shows your average yearly tax savings on a mortgage loan and calculates your after-tax interest rate on the loan. Loan closing costs, including mortgage points, are amortized over the term of the loan. Tax savings on a mortgage loan increase at higher income tax rates, all else remaining the same. This is because mortgage interest is generally tax deductible, reducing the after-tax interest rate.”[ix]

Quantitative Analysis:

Benchmark Model Client Scenarios

In order to test the quantitative aspects of complex mortgage calculators to determine if they produced valid results, a Model Client Scenario was created. All relevant major financial factors a prospective homeowner faces in determining the tax benefits of homeownership were taken into account when creating the Model Client Scenario. In order to reduce, if not eliminate, the unnecessary variability that is possible among individual transactions, all non-essential variables, including closing cost (closing and sales costs are negotiable and differ by locale) and the rate of property appreciation, are reduced to a value of zero (0).

The Model Client is analyzed from three perspectives: (1) as a renter, (2) as a buyer who finances the purchase transaction at 80% of the purchase price, and (3) as a buyer who pays the purchase price in full at closing without utilizing a bank product. The renter pays the Fair Rental Price for renting the property under consideration as described in greater detail below.

Given the Model Client Scenarios and the applicable tax code, the minimum inputs to yield the correct results were determined for the (mortgagor, renter and cash buyer) finance, rent & purchase scenarios, all else remaining constant. The minimum inputs consisted of (1) loan amount, (2) loan term, (3) interest rate, (4) state and federal tax rates, (5) property purchase price, (6) property taxes, (7) filing status, (8) the standard deduction for the given filing status, (9) an amount for rent that represents the fair rental price of the home being considered for purchase, and (10) a specific period of time.

The time period tested in every instance for either ownership or tenancy was 12 months. (This research recognizes that most homebuyers and mortgagors do not buy or mortgage their home on New Year's Eve or New Year's Day. Thus, they are unlikely to have a full twelve months of interest or property tax expense during the first year of homeownership.)

With the average price of a new home in the United States being in excess of $220,000 and the reported average range being $170,500 in the Midwest to a high of $349,000 in the West, a purchase price of $250,000 was used in the Model Client Scenario.

The loan amount chosen for the Model Client Finance Scenario was 80% of the Model Client Scenario purchase price or $200,000. Good credit is assumed. According to data from the Federal Reserve Board[x], commitments on 30 year fixed rate mortgages averaged 6.24% in November 2006. The interest rate used in the Model Client Scenario is 6.5%.

To allow for variations in the filing status of the individual, the Model Client Scenario allows for the following standard filing statuses: single, married filing separately, head of household and married filing jointly. The filing status tested is Married Filing Jointly.

The combined marginal tax rate used in the Model Client Scenario was a sum equal to the Social Security taxable wage base for 2006 of $94,200[xi], which makes the use of a federal and state marginal tax rate of 25% very reasonable regardless of filing status. The Model Client Scenario uses earned income and the associated marginal tax rates. No adjustments or calculations have been made to illustrate a changed source of income such as tax-free bond interest or long-term capital gains.

Summary of the Elements of the Model Client Scenario (Rent, Financed, Cash):

1) Gross income for the calendar year: $94,200.
2) Property Purchase Price/ Fair Market Value: $250,000
3) Fair Monthly Rental Price: $1,250.
4) Down Payment: Zero; $50,000; and $250,000.
5) Loan amount: Zero; $200,000; and zero.
6) Loan term: N/A, 30 years, N/A.
7) Interest rate: Zero/N/A; 6.5% and N/A.
8) Property taxes: Zero to 1% or $2,500 year
9) Property insurance: zero
10) Maintenance/Repairs: Zero to $2,500: 1% of property value (benefit of renting)
11) Other Allowable Expenses: Zero
12) Combined state and federal marginal tax rate: 25%
13) Filing status: Married Filing Jointly or Qualifying Widow (er)
14) The amount of the standard deduction for the given filing status: an acceptable value included the corresponding values for the 2004, 2005, or 2006 tax year.
15) Twelve (12) month time period.

Compute & Compare:

16) Compute and compare Dwelling Unit Expenses under each scenario.
17) Compute and compare Renting, financing the property with an 80% LTV based on the parameters above and purchasing the property for cash to the fair Rental Price of the property.
18) Compute and compare Imputed Rent under each scenario to Fair Rental Price.
19) Compute and compare the Mortgage Interest Deduction to the Standard Deduction under each scenario.
20) Compute and compare Dwelling Unit Expenses, cash flow and tax savings under each scenario.
21) Compute and compare the benefit associated with the omission of the Imputed Rent from adjusted gross income under each scenario.

Given the Model Client Rental Scenario, the benchmark dwelling unit expenses amount to $15,000 ($1,250 X 12), cash outlay $15,000, Mortgage Interest Deduction gross tax benefit of zero dollars and a net benefit after recognizing any difference attributable to any difference between the rent paid and fair market value of the property is zero. Given the Model Client Finance Scenario, the benchmark dwelling unit expenses amount to $17,934, cash outlay $20,170, Mortgage Interest Deduction gross tax benefit of $1,284 and a net benefit after recognizing the impact of the negative imputed rental value of $550. Given the Model Client Cash Scenario, the benchmark dwelling unit expenses amount to $5,000, cash outlay $5,000, Mortgage Interest Deduction gross tax benefit of zero and a net benefit after recognizing the benefit attributable to the positive imputed rental value of $2,500. These values served as the benchmark number by which the performance of all complex mortgage calculators examined were judged.

MODEL CLIENT SCENARIOS

	Scenario	Rent	Financed Purchase	Cash Purchase No Mortgage
	Gross Income			
1	Gross Income:	$94,200	$94,200	$94,200
	Purchase Price/Fair Market Value			
2	Purchase Price (PP):	$0	$250,000	$250,000
	Fair Rental Price (FRP)			
3	Fair Rental Price (FRP):	$15,000	$15,000	$15,000
	Down Payment			
4	Down Payment (DP):	$0	$50,000	$250,000
	Dwelling Unit Expenses (DUE)			
5	Property Taxes:	$0	$2,500	$2,500
6	Property Insurance:	$0	$0	$0
7	Maintenance & Repairs:	$0	$2,500	$2,500
8	Mortgage Interest Expense:	$0	$12,934	$0
9	Other Allowable Expenses:	$0	$0	$0
	Dwelling Unit Expense to Fair Rental Price			
10	Annualized Rent:	$15,000	$0	$0
11	Annualized Dwelling Unit Expense (ADUE):	$15,000	$17,934	$5,000
12	Annualized Dwelling Unit Expense to FRP:	100.00%	119.56%	33.33%
13	Annualized Cash Outlay (ACO):	$15,000	$20,170	$5,000
14	Annualized Cash Outlay to FRP:	100.00%	134.47%	33.33%
	Imputed Rent			
15	Imputed Rent (IR):	$0	-$2,934	$10,000
	Marginal Tax Rate			
16	Relevant Marginal Income Tax Rate:	25.00%	25.00%	25.00%
	Taxes Saved On Imputed Rent			
17	Tax Dollars Saved on Imputed Rent:	$0	-$734	$2,500
	Standard Deduction			
18	Relevant Standard Deduction: Zero Cost	$10,300	$10,300	$10,300
19	Standard Deduction Ratio to FRP:	68.67%	68.67%	68.67%
	Mortgage Interest Deduction			
20	Mortgage Interest Deduction Cost (MIDC):	$0	$15,434	$2,500
21	Mortgage Interest Deduction Cost to FRP:	0.00%	102.89%	16.67%
22	Annualized Tax Dollar Benefit of the MID:	$0	$1,284	$0
23	Net Dollar Benefit of the MID:	$0	$550	$0
24	Net Dollar Benefit of the MID to FRP:	0.00%	3.67%	0.00%
	Fair Rental Price (FRP) less Dwelling Unit Expenses (DUE)			
25	Dwelling Unit Expense Saved v. FRP:	$0	-$2,934	$10,000
	Dwelling Unit Expenses, Taxes, & Cash Flow Saved v. Fair Rental Price			
26	Dwelling Unit Expense Saved v. FRP:	$0	-$2,934	$10,000
27	Taxes Saved on Imputed Rent (IR):	$0	-$734	$2,500
28	Annualized Tax Dollar Benefit of the MID:	$0	$1,284	$0
29	DUE & Taxes Saved v. FRP:	$0	-$2,384	$12,500
30	DUE & Taxes Saved to FRP:	0.00%	-15.89%	83.33%
31	DUE, Taxes & Cash Flow Saved v. FRP:	$0	-$4,620	$12,500
32	DUE, Taxes & Cash Flow Saved to FRP:	0.00%	-30.80%	83.33%
	Principal Transfers			

Calculation of the Model Client's Mortgage Interest Deduction:

The calculation of tax savings (from the standpoint of the MID) starts with consideration of one year's mortgage interest (assuming a 12 month year) on the principal loan amount ($200,000) at the stated interest rate (6.5%) and term (30 years), which results in a sum certain of $12,934.18 in interest and $2,235.50 in principal. The amounts are rounded to the nearest dollar in the tables, $12,934 and $2,236 respectively.

Next comes the calculation of property taxes at 1% of the purchase price at $2,500 a year.

The combined sum of the mortgage interest and the property taxes, the amount that would be eligible for itemization under current tax law ($12,934 + $2,500) amounts to $15,434.

This sum $15,434 less the standard deduction for the Model Client Scenario – Married Filing Jointly - 2006 ($10,300) results in a net amount of = $5,134, this amount multiplied by the combined state and federal marginal tax rate of 25% ($5,134.18 *.25) = $1,283.50. The amount rounds out to $1,284 and represents a tax savings of $1,284 due to itemizing mortgage interest and property tax expense rather than taking the standard deduction.

Schedule Y-1 - If Your Filing Status is Married Filing Jointly or Qualifying Widow(er)

If your Taxable Income is: Over -	But Not Over -	The tax is:		Of the Amount over -
$0	$15,100	....	10%	0
$15,100	$61,300	$1,510.00 +	15%	$15,100
$61,300	$123,700	$8,440.00 +	25%	$61,300
$123,700	$188,450	$24,040.00 +	28%	$123,700

Source: IRS 2006 - 1040 Instructions, 2006 Tax Rate Schedule, Page 84

The figure $1,284 became the benchmark or index for the complex mortgage calculators examined in the study based on Schedule Y-1 as indicated above. Please note: If the 2006 tax tables are used instead of the tax schedule as indicated the index would be $1,275 instead of the $1,284, the dollar difference in using the tax tables and the tax schedule being $9. Again, given the Model Client Finance Scenario, the benchmark dwelling unit expenses amount to $17,934, cash outlay $20,170, Mortgage Interest Deduction gross tax benefit of $1,284 and a net benefit after recognizing the impact of the negative imputed rental value of $550. There is no benefit from the mortgage interest deduction for either the cash buyer or renter.

Part Four: Study Results

Quantitative Results:

From a population of 3,535 financial institutions, six hundred and seventy-five (674) banks were reviewed. Of those reviewed, five hundred and seventy-five (575) provided a simple calculator, while three hundred and seventy-six (376) state and federally chartered banks throughout the United States made complex Rent v. Buy and/or Save in Tax calculators available on or through their websites.

The Summary Table below shows each of the fifty states, the MSA for the state, along with the HHI market share for the banks reviewed, the market share of the banks within the MSA, and the percentage of DCMCs found within the banks reviewed.

Summary Table of Calculator Results by MSA (Part One)

	State	MSA	HHI Market Share	Mkt. Share of Banks Reviewed	DCMCs Found
1	Alabama	Birmingham	100%	88.56%	100%
2	Alaska	Anchorage	100%	99.99%	100%
3	Arizona	Phoenix	100%	89.12%	100%
4	Arkansas	Little Rock	100%	93.30%	100%
5	California	Los Angeles	100%	79.35%	100%
6	Colorado	Denver	100%	77.83%	100%
7	Connecticut	Bridgeport	100%	95.10%	100%
8	Delaware	Wilmington	100%	95.69%	100%
9	Florida	Jacksonville	100%	90.76%	100%
10	Georgia	Atlanta	100%	75.84%	100%
11	Hawaii	Honolulu	100%	98.73%	100%
12	Idaho	Boise City	100%	97.28%	100%
13	Illinois	Chicago	100%	66.25%	100%
14	Indiana	Indianapolis	100%	88.34%	100%
15	Iowa	Des Moines	100%	85.60%	100%
16	Kansas	Wichita	100%	83.47%	100%
17	Kentucky	Lexington	100%	58.74%	100%
18	Louisiana	New Orleans	100%	92.64%	100%
19	Maine	Portland	100%	96.23%	100%
20	Maryland	Baltimore	100%	81.33%	100%
21	Massachusetts	Boston	100%	76.94%	100%
22	Michigan	Detroit	100%	88.39%	100%
23	Minnesota	Minneapolis	100%	70.19%	100%
24	Mississippi	Jackson	100%	95.65%	100%
25	Missouri	Kansas City	100%	68.63%	100%

Legend	# Banks in MSA	Market Share of Banks Reviewed
Institutions Included in Market Share Concentration Study		
Total	3535	100%
Mean MSA	70.7	100%
Median MSA	45	100%
Range	5 – 305	100%
High	305	100%
Low	5	100%
Institutions Included in Individual MSA Review		
Total	674	
Mean MSA	13.48	88.80%
Median MSA	14	90.90%
Range	3 – 23	58-99%
High	23	99.99%
Low	3	58.74%

Summary Table of Calculator Results by MSA (Part Two)

	State	MSA	HHI Market Share	Mkt. Share of Banks Reviewed	DCMCs Found
26	Montana	Billings	100%	99.81%	100%
27	Nebraska	Omaha	100%	84.83%	100%
28	Nevada	Las Vegas	100%	92.24%	100%
29	New Hampshire	Manchester	100%	97.96%	100%
30	New Jersey	New York	100%	81.29%	100%
31	New Mexico	Albuquerque	100%	95.78%	100%
32	New York	New York	100%	81.29%	100%
33	North Carolina	Charlotte	100%	94.87%	100%
34	North Dakota	Fargo	100%	94.59%	100%
35	Ohio	Columbus	100%	90.37%	100%
36	Oklahoma	Oklahoma City	100%	81.24%	100%
37	Oregon	Portland	100%	91.03%	100%
38	Pennsylvania	Philadelphia	100%	80.97%	100%
39	Rhode Island	Providence	100%	93.97%	100%
40	South Carolina	Columbia	100%	94.36%	100%
41	South Dakota	Sioux Falls	100%	94.09%	100%
42	Tennessee	Memphis	100%	86.25%	100%
43	Texas	Houston	100%	81.83%	100%
44	Utah	Salt Lake City	100%	92.71%	100%
45	Vermont	Burlington	100%	99.30%	100%
46	Virginia	Virginia Beach	100%	94.98%	100%
47	Washington	Seattle	100%	86.35%	100%
48	West Virginia	Charleston	100%	96.79%	100%
49	Wisconsin	Milwaukee	100%	84.75%	100%
50	Wyoming	Cheyenne	100%	99.82%	100%

Legend	# Banks in MSA	Market Share of Banks Reviewed
Institutions Included in Market Share Concentration Study		
Total	3535	100%
Mean MSA	70.7	100%
Median MSA	45	100%
Range	5 - 305	100%
High	305	100%
Low	5	100%
Institutions Included in Individual MSA Review		
Total	674	
Mean MSA	13.48	88.80%
Median MSA	14	90.90%
Range	3 - 23	58-99%
High	23	99.99%
Low	3	58.74%

Inputs Varied on Mortgage Calculators Tested

The amount of data or inputs varied between mortgage calculators tested. Variations in style and layout from one bank website to another revealed that the number of possible inputs to the complex calculators ranged from eight to twenty. For example, the typical "Rent v. Own " mortgage calculator allowed for the following inputs: (1) Monthly rent, (2) monthly renter's insurance, (3) yearly rent increases, (4) purchase price, (5) appreciation rate, (6) savings rate, (7/8) state and/or federal tax rate, (9) the number of years before you sell the house or pay off the loan, (10) the loan amount, (11) the interest rate (no variation/allowance for adjustable rate product with varying rates), (12) discount points, (13) origination fee, (14) upfront costs, (15) yearly property taxes, (16) yearly maintenance, (17) yearly property insurance, (18) expected selling costs, (19) down payment and, (20) a savings rate.

All Cash Purchase Transactions Not Provided For In "Rent versus Buy" Calculation

All the calculators tested labeled "Rent versus Buy" did not allow for consideration of a 100% cash purchase of the home. "Rent versus Mortgage" may more aptly describe the calculation these calculators are presumed to make. Consideration of a "Rent versus Cash Buy" was not identified in the calculators tested or in the financial or marketing information appearing around or with the bank provided calculators.

Calculators Failed To Identify Quantifiable Benefits of Ownership v. Renting Absent a Mortgage

In an all cash home purchase, even though the purchaser does not receive tax savings from the mortgage interest deduction, a proper Rent versus Buy analysis should consider the savings related to (1) not paying rent and (2) no taxation on the "fair rental price" or the net rental value of the home. The tax benefit of not being taxed on the "fair rental price" of the home can be calculated and should be considered along with any other identified and related costs or benefits by anyone exploring the costs and benefits (contrasting) of renting versus buying a home.

While the financial and tax benefits of owning a home/house without a mortgage can be easily determined, it is important to note neither the financial benefits nor the tax benefit(s) of not having a mortgage is neither considered, nor weighed in the calculation, determination, or illustration of either the financial or tax benefits of renting versus buying a home by the calculators tested.

Calculators Failed To Identify Quantifiable Value (Fair Rental Rate/Price or Value) of The Property at Issue

Not one complex calculator out of 376 specifically identified or otherwise mentioned the Fair Rental Price of the home being compared or contrasted to a rental. The fair rental price/rate or value is "the amount of rent a person who is not related to you would be willing to pay."[xii] As a check on the amount, the IRS offers this, "The rent you charge is not a fair rental price if it is substantially less than the rents charged for other properties that are similar to your property."[xiii]

Calculators Failed To Identify The Downside of Paying Less Than A Fair Rental Rate or Price

Not one complex calculator out of 376 specifically identified or otherwise mentioned the downside of failing to pay rent equal to the Fair Market Rental Rate or Price.

Calculators Failed To Identify Any Imputed Rental Value Associated With the Property at Issue

Not one complex calculator out of 376 specifically identified or otherwise mentioned the Imputed Rental Value associated with any property being bought or rented.

Calculators Failed To Identify The Costs & Benefits Associated With Imputed Rental Value

Not one complex calculator out of 376 specifically identified or otherwise mentioned the benefits associated with Imputed Rental Value from the perspective of either a property owner or renter. For example, from the perspective of an owner, not one calculator mentioned the omission of imputed rent from adjusted gross income. The IRS refers to imputed rent in *Publication Number* 527 in relation to the (Fair Rental Price).

Using the model client, imputed rent or income is illustrated in three scenarios below. Column one illustrates renting. Column two illustrates financing the purchase with 20% down. Column three illustrates a 100% cash purchase.

The table below illustrates the tax treatment of the rent being equal to the fair rental price of a dwelling unit minus applicable expenses from the perspective of a renter, or an owner who made either a 20% or 100% down payment. The computations are useful in interpreting the significance of the results.

FAIR RENTAL PRICE & NET IMPUTED INCOME ILLUSTRATED

Exhibit One:

Scenario	**Renting**	**20% Down**	**100% Down**	Variance	**Variance** as a % of FRP
Total Annualized Cash Outlay *	$15,000	$20,170	$5,000	$15,170	101.10%
Dwelling Unit Expense **	$15,000	$17,934	$5,000	$12,934	86.22%
Fair Rental Price (FRP)	$15,000	$15,000	$15,000	0	0
Net Imputed Income * **	$0	$ -2,934	$10,000	$12,934	86.22%
Tax Benefit ******	$0	$ -734	$2,500	$3,234	21.56%

* Annualized cash outlay does not include the amount of the down payment.
** Dwelling unit expense does not include principal payment on the amortized loan.
*** Net Imputed Income is the dwelling unit expense minus the fair rental price.
**** Tax benefit is equal to Net Imputed Income multiplied by the applicable marginal tax rate.

In the above Exhibit One, four of the primary benefits of a mortgage free home are illustrated. One, there is a difference in total annualized cash outlay of $10,000 and $15,170 between being a renter or putting 20% down; two, there's a difference of $10,000 (renter) and $12,934 (20% down) in dwelling unit expenses for the same home; three, the net imputed income for the renter is zero, it's negative two thousand nine hundred and thirty-four dollars ($2,934) for the owner who put 20% down and it is $10,000 for the owner who has no mortgage; four, the tax benefit associated or connected with imputed rental value or income is zero for the renter; it's negative seven hundred and thirty-four dollars, -$734, for the 20% down owner and its $2,500 for the 100% down owner. These differences in values and benefits represent the economic advantage or benefit associated with being a homeowner without a mortgage.

It should be noted that in the above example and generally the benefit of the net rental value being excluded from an individual's adjusted gross income is a recognizable (primary) benefit of homeownership. This benefit is sensitive to the factors identified above (fair rental price & dwelling unit expenses), but as the individual's equity in the home grows, so does the benefit associated with the Fair Rental Price minus expenses (net rental value) not being taxed as part of the individual's Adjusted Gross Income (AGI).

In a market of stable or increasing rents the benefit would rise, as it would also increase gradually as a result of an amortized mortgage. This immediate increase in equity, and thus this immediate increase in the economic benefit associated with the imputed rental value, can be the result of either rising or stable rents coupled with debt reduction. Property appreciation can be positive or negative and can move independently from rents. For these reasons, property appreciation was held to zero in the Model Client Scenario and rent was assumed stable for the period indicated. The loan, however, was amortized over a thirty-year period.

Complex Calculators Consistently Overstated Benefits of the MID

The complex (Rent v. Buy and/or Tax Savings) calculators tested overstated the benchmark tax benefits that the model client would receive by $2,575, showing on average $3,859 in tax benefit when the benchmark benefit amounted to $1,284 (all figures rounded to the nearest dollar). Hence, for the model client, the expected tax benefit was overstated by as much as 300% ($3,859/$1,284).

This study found that none (zero) of the complex mortgage calculator out of the 376 tested accurately calculated the tax benefits associated with the mortgage interest deduction for the Model Client Scenario.

While the benchmark tax savings based on the Model Client Scenario is $1,284 rounded to the nearest dollar, if the filing status were other than that used in the Model Client Scenario, for example single or head of household for 2006, the following result would be expected versus the standard deduction for the given filing status:

A) Benchmark tax savings amount to $2,571.05 for a filing status of **Single or Married Filing Separately** for 2006 assuming mortgage interest and property taxes of $15,434.18 minus the standard deduction for this filing status during 2006 of $5,150 multiplied by the model client's assumed combined state and federal tax rate of 25% ($15,434.18 – $5,150) * 0.25 = $2,571.05

B) Benchmark tax savings amount to $1,971.05 for a filing status of **Head of Household** for 2006 assuming mortgage interest and property taxes of $15,434.18 minus the standard deduction for this filing status during 2006 of $7,550 multiplied by the model client's assumed combined state and federal tax rate of 25% ($15,434.18 – $7,550) * 0.25 = $1,971.05

C) Benchmark tax savings amount to $1,283.55 for a filing status of **Married Filing Jointly** for 2006 assuming mortgage interest and property taxes of $15,434.18 minus the standard deduction for this filing status during 2006 of $10,300 multiplied by the model client's assumed combined state and federal tax rate of 25% ($15,534.18 – $10,300) * 0.25 = $1,283.50

Please note: For taxpayers who are age 65 or older or who are blind, the standard deduction is higher. For example, in 2006, the standard deduction is increased $1,000 for the aged and for the blind ($1,250 if single). Hence, if the model client scenario couple were in their mid-sixties and blind the Standard Deduction would increase from $10,300 to $14,300. The expected value of the Mortgage Interest Deduction would be ($15,534.18 - $14,300) * .25 = $308.50. The amount is increased to $1,250 if the individual is also unmarried and not a surviving spouse.

In addition to the other results and flaws already identified, one of the major consistent flaws in the complex mortgage calculators tested was that they did not consider the standard deduction to which the taxpayer maybe entitled. To further illustrate this flaw, if the complex mortgage calculator does not take into account the standard deduction, it will calculate tax savings for taxpayers even though the taxpayer will derive no tax benefit if the MID and other itemized deductions do not exceed the standard deduction, as in the all Cash Model Client Scenario.

Other Considerations Not Taken Into Account In Rent v. Buy Calculations

Rent, buy, or rent versus buy analysis most often fail to ask how much can the buyer afford to put down on a house (0-100%), how much can the buyer afford to spend on housing on a regular basis (monthly), and what is the regular source of the buyer's income. If a buyer can put 100% down, they may not need financing. How much the buyer can afford to spend takes into account what's available and what one can expect the cost differences to be between renting and buying. The two principal differences in monthly or annual costs are maintenance expenses and property taxes. These two expenses are generally absent in a rental situation. Utilities may or may not be included in rent, although water is typically included in rent. Utilities in general tend to be higher (based on census data) on owner occupied properties versus renter occupied property. The source and amount of a buyer's income in addition to any dollar expenditures for utilities, property taxes, maintenance and even furnishings can impact total housing costs.

It's been suggested that in order to determine how much house a buyer can afford, one should take into consideration four issues: monthly cash flow, cash reserves or savings, future monthly housing expenses, and purchase cost.[xiv] It is also suggested that before a buyer looks for a home he/she should determine how much can be spent on the home monthly, how much he/she can afford to spend on a down payment, and the costs involved in closing, then analyze present spending and saving patterns inclusive of monthly income, monthly non-housing expenses and monthly housing expenses present and proposed.

Given the model client scenario in calculating costs, a major question becomes does the source of funds used to pay for housing impact the cost of housing for a given period of time?

Does it make a difference whether one buys or rents for a given period of time?

?? Given the source of funds being earned income.
?? Given the source of funds being unearned income.
?? Given unearned income from tax-free bonds.
?? Given unearned income from Long-term capital gain.
?? Given unearned income from Dividends.
?? Given unearned income from Interest.

The two largest expenses in the household budget are generally housing and transportation costs. When deciding housing costs, the individual should not only take the expected difference in utilities, property taxes and insurance into consideration, but also any additional transportation costs. HUD and the Bureau of the Census have long been aware that those who live in urban and suburban areas have different commutes and transportation expenses. Some new proposed housing indexes, e.g., Brooking Institute and MIT[xv], are giving consideration to transportation, quality of public school, access to employment, and environmental conditions as it is believed that some of these costs are not reflected in the current price of housing and thus housing comparison costs.

Results of the Herfindahl-Hirschman Index of Market Concentration

The Herfindahl-Hirschman Index (HHI) of market concentration is provided for the largest MSA in each state based upon the banking institutions in the marketplace (3,535) and the market share of deposits they actually hold. The number of financial institutions (pre-merger) in a MSA ranged from a low of five (5 - Alaska) to a high of three hundred and five (305 - Chicago) and the average MSA has 71 financial institutions. Summary data is presented here based on three different market concentrations. Based on an MSA's HHI, the three market concentrations are: (1) the Unconcentrated Market (UCM) for those MSA that have an initial HHI of 1,000 points or less; (2) the Moderately Concentrated Market (MCM) made up of those MSAs with HHI of between 1,000 and 1,800 points; and (3) the Highly Concentrated Market (HCM) made up of those MSAs whose HHI exceeded 1,800 points.

The website examinations then takes place of those banking institutions (identified individually by name, market share, FDIC # and by HHI points) in each market concentration in each MSA that had a 1% or greater market share. Those banking institutions that made a Rent v. Buy (RvB) calculator available on or through their website are further identified and the performance of the calculator is given.

Data is summarized in this section of the report, but all MSAs are listed in the Appendix alphabetically by state and MSA, and in tables from lowest to highest based on such factors as Market Share, Actual HHI for MSA, Actual HHI for Banks Reviewed, Point Difference Between Initial & Pro-Forma HHI, MSA Number of Institutions Reviewed (1%ers), Ranked by # of Institutions (1%ers) w/ RvB Calculators, Ranked by Pro-Forma HHI (lowest to highest), etc.

This page is intentionally blank

The Unconcentrated Banking Market

Thirteen (13) MSAs exist in what is classified as the Unconcentrated Banking Market with a HHI range from 408.4852 (Kansas City) to 969.6851 (Birmingham) points and a mean HHI of 771.03364 as indicated in the figure #1 below.

Fig. # 1	Unconcentrated Market (UCM)			
	MSA Actual HHI	MSA Pro Forma HHI	MSA Mkt. Share	# of Banks in MSAs
Mean	771.0336	3240.7848	100.00%	109
Median	781.4255	3175.5565	100.00%	86

The mean market share of those banking institutions with 1% or greater market share in those 13 MSAs in the UCM is over 81% as indicated in figure #2 below. The mean number of institutions in each MSA drops from 109 to a little more than 17 when the focus is on the 1%ers. As would be expected, the HHI dropped from a mean just above 771 (figure #1) to 762 (figure #2) for this smaller group, but the old 80-20 rule appears to be in play, as this group of 17 institutions make up less than 16% of the institutions in the UCM, but they control more than 80% of the depository market. Chicago was the MSA with the lowest market share at 66.25% in the UCM and Lexington at 93.43% edged out Little Rock at 93.30% as the MSA with the largest market share in the UCM.

Fig. # 2	Unconcentrated Market (UCM)		
	1%ers Actual HHI	1%ers Actual Mkt. Share	# of 1%ers in MSA
Mean	762.183	81.30%	17.31
Median	776.9679	81.24%	17
Std. Dev.	155.9298	8.11%	3.25

Upon closer examination on the 13 MSAs in the Unconcentrated Bank Market (UCM), those 1% percenters who had RvB calculators had a mean Actual HHI of 617 points [see. Fig. # 3 below], but on a Pro-Forma basis their HHI jumped by more 2,398 points to a mean of 3,015 points [see Fig. # 3]. The 2,398-point jump is more than 23X the 100-point jump that should begin to raise eyebrows and competitive concerns. Less than 8% of the companies in the UCM control more than 54% of the market (less than 9 banks 1%ers [fig. # 3] out of an average of 109 banks [fig.#1] in the UCM). Less than nine banks expose more than 54% of the UCM bank market to Defective Complex Mortgage Calculators. The MSA with the lowest market share of RvB Calculators in the UCM bank market is Baltimore (41.73%) and MSA with the highest is Little Rock (71.75%). The Pro-Forma HHI mean for all 13 MSAs (approx. 1417 institutions) in the UCM jumped from 771 to 3240 or 2,469 points (See Fig. # 1. above).

Fig. # 3

	Unconcentrated Market (UCM)			
	RvB Actual HHI	RvB Pro Forma HHI	RvB Market Share	# of 1%ers w/RvB
Mean	617.1357	3015.4146	54.28%	8.77
Median	647.6083	2992.09	54.70%	8
Std. Dev.	144.1045	989.8912	8.67%	2.65

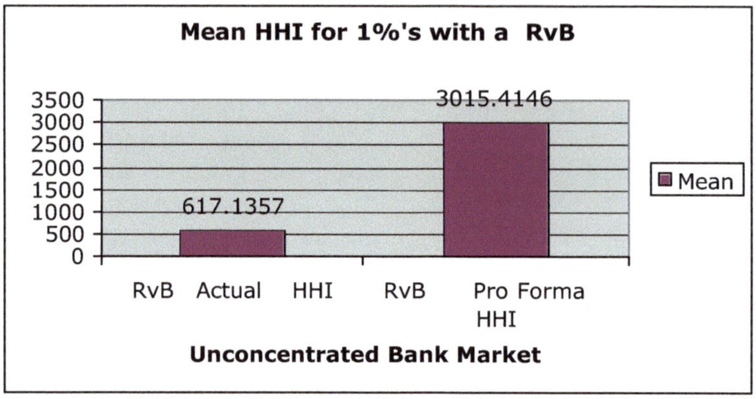

The Moderately Concentrated Bank Market

In contrast to the UCM, the number of MSAs qualifying for the Moderately Concentrated Banking Market (MCM) doubled to twenty-six (26) as the qualifying HHI point range on the low end is 1,000 points and begins with 1,105.831 in the New Jersey/ New York MSA and tops out at 1,800 HHI points on the high end. The closet of the 26 MSAs without going over is Wilmington with a HHI of 1,741.974 points. The mean Actual HHI for all 26 MSAs in the MCM is 1378.391 points as indicated in figure #4 in the table below. It's worth noting that while the number of MSA in the Moderately Concentrated Market doubled the mean number of banking institutions in each of the MSAs dropped from 109 to 69 or by 36.6%.

Fig. # 4	Moderately Concentrated Market (MCM)			
	MSA Actual HHI	MSA Pro Forma HHI	MSA Mkt. Share	# of Banks in MSAs
Mean	1378.391	5023.6532	100.00%	69
Median	1350.481	5037.98	100.00%	43

Although the mean MSA in the Moderately Concentrated Market had 69 banking institutions, the mean number of institutions in an MSA that have 1% or more of the market is 13.73 or 20% of the average number of institutions in a MCM MSA, but they account for a whopping 90.03% of the market share (see Fig. # 5 below). The median market share is actually higher than the mean at 91.84%. The range is a low of 70.19% in Minneapolis with seven banking institutions to 99.81% in Billings being runner up to Cheyenne with a 99.82% market share based on fifteen institutions, but the end of the range for the number of banking institutions with a 1% or greater market share in the MCM was a five way tie at 17 (Newark/New York, Houston, Milwaukee, and New Orleans). The mean Actual HHI for the 1%ers was 1,379.94 points (See fig.# 5 below).

Fig. # 5	Moderately Concentrated Market		
	1%ers Actual HHI	1%ers Actual Mkt. Share	# of 1%ers in MSA
Mean	1379.94	90.03%	13.73
Median	1342.975	91.84%	15.00
Std. Dev.	189.2381	7.47%	2.88

The Moderately Concentrated Banking Market (Continued)

Examining the 1%ers in the 26 MSAs that make up the MCM reveals that on average eight institutions control more than 68% of the market and expose more than 68% of the banking market to defective RvB calculators (see Fig. # 6 below). These banking institutions (1% percenters) who make RvB calculators available on or through their websites had a mean Actual HHI of 1,159.9375 points [see. Fig. # 6 below], which as expected is below the 1,373.94 points for the mean MSA in the MCM but, on a Pro-Forma basis their HHI jumped by more 3,633.2904 points to 4,793.2279. A 3,633-point jump is more than 36 times the 100-point benchmark. From the standpoint of range on the number of 1%ers with RvB calculators and by market share, you have Billings at the low end with three institutions with a 39.82% market share and Newark/New York and Indianapolis tied based on the number of institutions with RvB Calculators available with twelve being the number, but Columbus leading the MCM MSA market with RvB calculator exposure of 85.06%.

	Moderately Concentrated Market			
Fig. # 6	RvB Actual HHI	RvB Pro Forma HHI	RvB Market Share	# of 1%ers w/RvB
Mean	1159.938	4793.2279	68.39%	8.04
Median	1178.3	4844.8941	69.61%	8
Std. Dev.	280.4466	1429.2541	11.00%	2.55

The 26 MSAs in the moderately concentrated banking markets had a mean HHI of 1378.3865 that became a mean HHI of 5023.653 on a pro-forma basis. To give you some perspective, remember that the HHI went down as expected when looking at the average HHI in the MSA generally at 1,378 points and the 1%ers at 1,159 points, a drop of over 219 points. On a pro-forma basis, there is over a 3,6343 point increase or spread in HHI in the wrong direction.

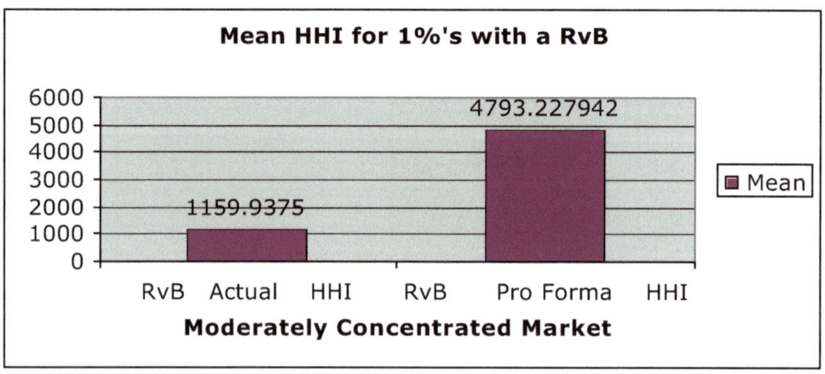

The Highly Concentrated Banking Market

Please note, the actual HHI point difference between the 1%ers in an MSA and the MSA HHI on average is less than 14 points overall for all MSAs and the range is .0001 - 13.7041.

The highly concentrated bank market has the smallest number of MSAs (11), the lowest mean number of banking institutions in each MSA (31), the lowest mean number of institutions with 1% or greater market share (8.36), the lowest mean number of institutions with RvB calculators (4.82), the lowest mean point difference between an MSA and the 1%ers (2.646), the highest mean actual HHI of all markets at 3,384.836 points, the highest mean market share among 1%ers at 94.78%, and the highest mean pro-forma HHI of any MSA at 5,158.877 (Please see fig. 7, 8 & 9 below.)

Fig. # 7

	Highly Concentrated Market			
	MSA Actual HHI	MSA Pro Forma HHI	MSA Mkt. Share	# of Banks in MSAs
Mean	3384.836	6019.4273	100.00%	31
Median	2875.814	5983.8658	100.00%	33

Fig. # 8

	Highly Concentrated Market		
	1%ers Actual HHI	1%ers Actual Mkt. Share	# of 1%ers in MSA
Mean	3382.19	94.78%	8.36
Median	2875.443	94.87%	7
Std. Dev.	1851.605	4.17%	3.56

Fig. # 9

	Highly Concentrated Market			
	RvB Actual HHI	RvB Pro Forma HHI	RvB Market Share	# of 1%ers w/RvB
Mean	2524.533	5158.877	66.96%	4.82
Median	2209.66	5478.9604	74.02%	5
Std. Dev.	2289.53	3054.7949	27.24%	2.27

This page is intentionally blank

Other Deficient Complex Mortgage Calculators Discovered

(1) The Government National Mortgage Association (GNMA or Ginnie Mae) Website Provides Access To A Deficient Complex Mortgage Calculator

Ginnie Mae is a federally owned corporation within the Department of Housing and Urban Development (HUD). Ginnie Mae (pioneered the mortgage backed securities market) securities are the only mortgaged-backed securities that have the full faith and credit guaranty of the United States Government (e.g., FHA, VA, RHA, PIH), as they say, they "help make affordable housing a reality for millions of households across America". HUD suggests that the first thing a prospective homebuyer should do is figure out how much they can afford. "What you can afford depends on your credit rating, current monthly expenses, down payment and interest rate. The calculators below (How much home can you afford and Buying vs. Renting) can help, but it is best to visit a lender to find out for sure."[xvi]

The HUD website suggested the use of two calculators. The two calculators are "How Much Home Can You Afford" and "Buying vs. Renting." The "Buying vs. Renting" calculator link on HUD's website takes you to a "Buying vs. Renting" calculator on Ginnie Mae's website. The calculator only allows the user to input: (1) current rent, (2) purchase price of home, (3) percentage of down payment, (4) length of loan terms, (5) interest rate, (6) years you plan to stay in this home, (7) yearly property tax rate and (8) yearly home value increase rate and then either the refresh or calculate button[xvii].

Information based upon the model client was entered into the Ginnie Mae complex mortgage calculator (CMC), "Buy vs. Rent Calculator". The calculated results or tax savings based on the Ginnie Mae provided CMC was $4,340. The model client tax savings should have been $1,284. The benefits per the Ginnie Mae provided CMC are over stated by $3,056. The benefit illustrated by the Ginnie Mae provided CMC overstates the actual benefit by 338% ($4,340/$1,284).

Based on the findings of this study, the information provided in this first step suggested by HUD can lead prospective homebuyers to the wrong conclusion in determining how much house they can afford as a result of the deficient complex mortgage calculator used in making that determination. U.S. Financial Literacy & Education Commission also links to this site.

(2) The Federal Home Loan Mortgage Corporation (Freddie Mac) Website Provides Access To A Deficient Complex Mortgage Calculator

Freddie Mac is a corporation that purchases both conventional and federally insured first mortgages from members of the federal reserve system and other approved banks. Freddie Mac's "Rent vs. Buy" calculator is introduced using the question "Am I better off renting?" The calculator allows as many as eighteen (18) inputs. The monthly mortgage (P&I) payment was calculated correctly at $1,264. The benefit of owning over renting is calculated incorrectly at saving $6,424 by owning over renting. Total tax savings are calculated incorrectly at $3,859. Again the tax savings benchmark is $1,284. Thus the illustrated benefit to the benchmark benefit is $3,859/$1,284 or 3.00 times greater than the benchmark benefit (300% over stated and a dollar difference of $2,575 over the benchmark benefit. The calculator vendor is Lead Fusion. A visit to the Federal National Mortgage Association (FNMA or Fannie Mae) website found a CMC, but it focuses on payment and affordability (Proprietary calculator), no rent v. buy comparison.

(3) The Mortgage Professor Website Provides Access to A Deficient Complex Mortgage Calculator

The "Mortgage Professor" a.k.a. Jack M. Guttentag (Professor of Finance Emeritus at the Wharton School of the University of Pennsylvania and founder of GHR Systems, Inc., a mortgage technology company) provides access to calculator 8a[xviii] (Amortization Schedule Including Tax Savings) on his website that claims the calculator is for those "Borrowers who want an amortization schedule that shows the tax savings on interest they pay, for their tax bracket" and that "this calculator shows the amortization schedule including tax savings at a specified tax bracket." The calculator allows an individual to enter (1) loan amount or balance, (2) interest rate, (3) loan term, (4) rate on savings, and (5) income tax bracket. Given the model client data, the Mortgage Professor's Calculators determined the accumulated tax savings over the first twelve months amounted to $3,234 rounded to the nearest dollar. Again, the benchmark tax benefit to the model client is $1,284. Thus, the illustrated benefit to the benchmark benefit is $3,234/$1,284 or 2.518 times (252%) greater than the benchmark benefit and a dollar difference of $1,950 over the benchmark benefit.

(4) The SmartMoney.com Website Provides Access To A Deficient Complex Mortgage Calculator

The SmartMoney.com website's "To Rent or To Buy?[xix]" calculator states that things being equal it's almost always better to own your home rather than to rent. Stating, "After all, you build equity *and* get to write off your mortgage interest. And if you play your cards right, when you sell you'll be eligible for one of the best tax breaks around. But that doesn't mean that everyone should be a homeowner. If your move is short-term or if interest rates are high and property values deteriorating, it may be worthwhile to deal with a landlord for a while. Our worksheet will help you determine which path is best."

A side bar states – "Choosing whether to rent or buy is a complicated and sometimes emotional decision. This worksheet can't tell you the right answer, but it will help you compare renting and buying as investment strategies. When you buy, you build equity with every monthly payment. But when you rent, you typically pay less each month and don't need to scrape together a down payment - which leaves more money to put in your portfolio. Our worksheet will estimate how much value you'll build in each case."

The SmartMoney worksheet allowed the user to input 12 values and adjust the value within set parameters on a 13th variable. The monthly mortgage payment was calculated at $1,264. The average monthly mortgage payment net interest deduction was calculated at $995 implying a difference of $269 a month or $3,228 a year. Again, the benchmark tax benefit to the model client is $1,284. Thus, the illustrated benefit to the benchmark benefit is $3,228/$1,284 or 2.51 times greater (251%) than the benchmark benefit and a dollar difference of $1,944 over the benchmark benefit.

(5) The American Bankers Association Website Provides Access To A Deficient Complex Mortgage Calculator

The American Bankers Association website (aba.com) is sponsored by the Corporation for American Banking, LLC. If you click on the site sponsor link it takes you to the home page for the Corporation for American Banking, which tells you that it is an ABA subsidiary and that they identify and sponsors products and services that assist banks with their income-producing, efficiency, operational, and competitive needs.[xx] On the ABA Mortgage Lending Solutions and Resources page, it states that the "ABA offers members a wide variety of mortgage and real estate lending solutions and products. Secondary Market partnerships with Fannie Mae and Freddie Mac give you a competitive advantage in mortgage lending; calculators help you and your customers know what loans are right for them".[xxi] On that same page, under the heading of additional resources and just under the links to Fannie Mae and Freddie Mac is a link entitled "Should You Rent or Buy?"[xxii]

Clicking on "Should You Rent or Buy?" brings up a page with a heading that reads "American Bankers Association aba.com Financial Education" and a sub heading of "Rent vs. Buy Calculator"[xxiii]. The claim; "This calculator will compare the costs of renting vs. the real cost of buying a home. This calculator will compare the costs and benefits of taxes, fees, and interest you will pay when buying a home to the monthly rent you pay when renting. It does not include payments made against the principal on your loan, since those payments become equity in your home." The calculator allows an individual to enter data on up to (17) seventeen different items. Given the model client data, the calculators determined that the net cost of renting was $15,000 and the net cost of buying was $11,575.64 stating that, "You will save $3,424.36 if you buy instead of rent." Again, the benchmark tax benefit to the model client is $1,284 before adjusting for a negative imputed rental value. Hence, on the basis of the Mortgage Interest Deduction alone, the benefit is overstated by $3,411 or 266% or while renting was going to cost $1,250 a month, buying would result in a net costs of $964.63 a month.

The bottom of the page states that "Presented by Time Value Software for the American Bankers Association." In an approximately 6.5 Helvetica font it states that:

> "The information provided by these calculators is for illustrative purposes only. The information entered may vary from your actual loan, mortgage, investment, or savings results. Interest rates are hypothetical and are not meant to represent any specific investment. Rates of return will vary over time, particularly for long-term investments. The calculated results are not guaranteed to be accurate and are in no way endorsed, offered or guaranteed by American Bankers Association."

This page is intentionally blank

Qualitative Results

FTC ACT

Title 15 U.S.C § 45 (a)(1) states that, "Unfair methods of competition in or affecting commerce, and unfair or deceptive acts or practices in or affecting commerce are declared unlawful." The next paragraph states that the Federal Trade Commission (FTC) is "empowered and directed to prevent persons, partnerships, or corporations, except banks, saving and loan institutions described in section 57 a (f)(3)...from using unfair methods of competition in or affecting commerce and unfair or deceptive acts or practices in or affecting commerce."[xxiv]

Section 57a(f)(3), focuses on rule making proceedings as it relates to unfair or deceptive acts or practices by banks, savings and loan institutions, among others and specifies that, "in order to prevent unfair or deceptive acts or practices in or affecting commerce (including acts or practices which are unfair or deceptive to consumers) by banks or savings and loan institutions each agency...shall establish a separate division of consumer affairs which shall receive and take appropriate action...by banks and savings and loan institutions...subject to its jurisdiction. The board of Governors of the Federal Reserve System (with respect to banks) and the Federal Home Loan Bank Board (with respect to savings and loan associations)...shall prescribe regulations to carry out the purposes of this section, including regulations defining with specificity such unfair acts or deceptive acts or practices, and containing requirements prescribed for the purpose of preventing such acts or practices."[xxv] Compliance with these regulations is enforced under section 1818 of title 12, in the case of national banks by the division of consumer affairs established by the Office of the Comptroller of the Currency; members of the Federal Reserve System (other than national banks) by the division of consumer affairs established by the Board of Governors of the Federal Reserve System; and for banks insured by the federal Deposit Insurance Corporation (FDIC) by the division of consumer affairs established by the Board of Directors of the federal Deposit Insurance Corporation.

Federal Reserve & FDIC Joint Statement

On March 11, 2004, the Board of Governors of the Federal Reserve System and the Federal Deposit Insurance Corporation issued a joint statement reinforcing previous pronouncements (May 2002) and outlining the standards that they will consider as they carry out their responsibilities to enforce prohibitions against unfair or deceptive trade practices found in section 5 of the Federal Trade Commission Act (FTC Act) when weighing the need to take supervisory and enforcement actions and when seeking to ensure that unfair or deceptive practices do not recur by state-chartered banks as they affirmed their authority under section 8 of the Federal Deposit Insurance Act to take appropriate action when unfair or deceptive acts or practices are discovered.[xxvi]

This page is intentionally blank

Deceptive Act or Practices Defined

The Federal Trade Commission, along with most state statues and Black's Law Dictionary, define a "deceptive act" as conduct that is likely to deceive a consumer acting reasonably under the circumstances.

The Board and the FDIC acknowledged that a representation, omission, or practice is deceptive "if it is likely to mislead a consumer acting reasonably under the circumstances and is likely to affect a consumer's conduct or decision regarding a product or service."[xxvii] In assessing whether and act or practice is deceptive, they employ a three part test: "First, the representation, omission, or practice must mislead or be likely to mislead the consumer. Second, the consumer's interpretation of the representation, omission, or practice must be reasonable under the circumstances. Lastly, the misleading representation, omission, or practice must be material."[xxviii]

The Board and the FDIC agree "a representation, omission, or practice is material if it is likely to affect a consumer's decision regarding a product or service. In general, information about costs, benefits, or restrictions on the use or availability of a product or service is material. When express claims are made with respect to a financial product or service, the claims will be presumed to be material. Similarly, the materiality of an implied claim will be presumed when it is demonstrated that the institution intended that the consumer draw certain conclusions based upon the claim. Claims made with the knowledge that they are false will also be presumed to be material. Omissions will be presumed to be material when the financial institution knew or should have known that the consumer needed the omitted information to evaluate the product or service."[xxix] "Withholding material price information until after the consumer has committed to purchase the product or service would be an example of preventing a consumer from making an informed decision."[xxx]

Unfair Act or Practice Defined

Regulators have determined that an act or practice can be deceptive without also being unfair and thus the standards for deception and unfairness are independent of each other. In determining if an act or practice is unfair, regulators once again look to the principles applied by the Federal Trade Commission. Once again, the Board and the FDIC mutually agree that an act or practice is unfair "where it (1) causes or is likely to cause substantial injury to consumers, (2) cannot be reasonably avoided by consumers, and (3) is not outweighed by countervailing benefits to consumers or to competition."[xxxi]

As it relates to substantial injury, the Board and the FDIC point out that emotional distress and other subjective types of harms will not ordinarily make a practice unfair and that trivial and speculative harms are generally insufficient for a finding of substantial injury, but an injury may be substantial if it raises a significant risk of concrete harm and they find that a substantial risk usually involves a monetary harm, although an act or practice that causes a small amount of harm to a large number of people may be deemed a substantial injury.

While rent versus buy decisions can be emotional, there should be little doubt that both the rental or purchase of housing involves money and although the sums can vary, a single rental or purchase generally involves thousands of dollars and a single institution can subject hundreds or thousands of individuals to unfair and/or deceptive acts or practices that can be both easy and costly to get into and costly to get out of and while the Board and the FDIC will also look at the net effect of an act or practice as it relates to both the consumer and competition they will not second-guess the wisdom of particular consumer decisions, but they will consider "whether a bank's behavior unreasonably creates or takes advantage of an obstacle to the free exercise of consumer decision making."[xxxii].

However, since one of the goals of this report was to challenge the HUD-Treasury Report and conventional thinking in relation to predatory lending practices, it's important to point out that the general description of predatory lending in the HUD-Treasury report was, "engaging in deception or fraud, manipulating the borrower through aggressive sales tactics, or taking advantage of a borrower's lack of understanding about loan terms" [xxxiii]. While the generally accepted definition of "manipulating", "aggressive sales tactics" and "lack of understanding" is sufficient for this report, because the Board and the FDIC have taken the time to clarify the difference between "deceptive" and "unfair" acts and practices and HUD and the Treasury Department have provided a definition of "predatory lending" as engaging in either "deception" or "fraud", for the sake of clarification I provide the definition of fraud as found in Black's Law Dictionary: (1) A knowing misrepresentation of the truth or concealment (nondisclosure) of a material fact (or at least misleading conduct, devices, or contrivance) to induce another to act to his or her detriment[xxxiv].

The OCC has taken enforcement action in situations where it found a national bank's practices were deceptive. In each instance, the practice at issue involved a representation or omission about a material aspect of a product or service that was misleading including: a) failure to provide sufficient information to allow a consumer to understand the terms of the product or service being offered without being misled; b) failure to adequately disclose when significant fees or similar material prerequisites applied in order to obtain the particular product or service being offered; and c) failure to disclose material limitations affecting the product or service being offered.

Part Five: Implications and Applications

Observations and Opinions From A - Z

What follows is a short, and not all-inclusive list of some of the primary observations and opinions made during the course of this study:

(a) A reasonable consumer would believe that a Rent v. Buy (RvB) calculator made available for use on or through their bank's website was capable of doing what it claimed/purported to do.

(b) A reasonable consumer would believe that a Save in Tax (SiTx) calculator and/or any other calculator made available for use on or through their bank's website was capable of doing what calculators do.

(c) A reasonable consumer would believe that a Rent v Buy, calculations or results would be valid.

(d) A reasonable consumer would believe that a Save in Tax calculations or results would be valid.

(e) While RvB and SiTx calculators allowed for as many as twenty inputs, they consistently omitted an address line or failed to allow for insertion of a property's specific address.

(f) RvB and SiTx calculators consistently omitted any reference to an individual's specific credit report or profile.

(g) RvB and SiTx calculators failed to mention (or otherwise omitted mentioning) the fair rental price of the property being compared/contrasted.

(h) RvB and SiTx calculators failed to mention (or otherwise omitted mentioning) the tax pros and cons associated with the fair rental price.

(i) RvB and SiTx calculators failed to mention (or otherwise omitted mentioning) anything about imputed rent, imputed rental income or value and the pros and cons associated with imputed rent, imputed rental income or value.

(j) The difference between the fair rental price and the imputed rental value was even (or zero) for the renting model client.

(k) The difference between the fair rental price and the imputed rental value was a negative number for our model client who financed the purchase of a home.

(l) The difference between the fair rental price and the imputed rental value was a positive number or value for the model client that put 100% down.

This page is intentionally blank

(m) An RvB and SiTx calculator's failure to mention either the fair rental price or the tax pros and cons associated with the fair rental price and imputed rental value could influence a reasonable consumer's decision to rent a home.

(n) An RvB and SiTx calculator's failure to mention either the fair rental price or the tax pros and cons associated with the fair rental price and imputed rental value could influences a reasonable consumers decision to purchase a home.

(o) An RvB and SiTx calculator's failure to mention either the fair rental price or the tax pros and cons associated with the fair rental price and imputed rental value could influence a reasonable consumers decision to finance a home.

(p) An RvB and SiTx calculator's failure to accurately calculate but regularly and consistently overstate the benefits and values (but not the limitations) associated with the Mortgage Interest Deduction could influence a reasonable consumer's decision about renting a home.

(q) An RvB and SiTx calculator's failure to accurately calculate but regularly overstate the benefits associated with the Mortgage Interest Deduction could influence a reasonable consumer's decision to purchase a home.

(r) An RvB and SiTx calculator's failure to accurately calculate but regularly overstate the benefits associated with the Mortgage Interest Deduction could influence a reasonable consumer's decision to finance a home.

(s) An RvB and SiTx calculator's failure to recognize an individual's primary source of income could influence a reasonable consumer's decision to rent a home.

(t) An RvB and SiTx calculator's failure to recognize an individual's primary source of income could influence a reasonable consumer's decision to purchase a home.

(u) An RvB and SiTx calculator's failure to recognize an individual's primary source of income could influence a reasonable consumer's decision to finance a home.

(v) A reasonable consumer wouldn't expect their bank (or a mainstream bank) to make a faulty Save in Tax calculator available on or through their website as a way of originating more mortgage loans.

(w) A reasonable consumer wouldn't expect their bank (or a mainstream bank) to make a faulty Rent v. Buy calculator available on or through their website as a way of originating more mortgage loans.

(x) A reasonable consumer wouldn't expect their bank (or a mainstream bank) to use technology against them in order to originate more mortgage loans.

(y) A reasonable consumer wouldn't expect their bank (or a mainstream bank) to use the law against them in order to originate more mortgage loans.

(z) A reasonable consumer wouldn't expect their bank to use faulty mortgage calculators, technology, the law, public practice or self-help personal financial planning, and/or America's general apparent inability to readily distinguish between educational and marketing material to originate more mortgage loans.

Disclaimer & Disclosures

A disclaimer is defined as, "1. A renunciation of One's legal right or claim. 2. A repudiation of another's legal right or claim. 3. A writing that contains such a renunciation or repudiation."[xxxv]

The calculators tested during this study frequently posted a disclaimer regarding the accuracy of the results. However, due to a bank's name and reputation, a consumer may not expect the calculator to be off by a significant amount or that some basic tax and financial considerations wouldn't be taken into account or disclosed.

In contrast to a disclaimer, disclosure is defined as, "the act or process of making known something that was previously unknown; a revelation of facts."[xxxvi] Given the widespread errors found during the testing of these Rent v. Buy and Save In Tax mortgage calculators, it was discovered that some banks (have no problem) disclosing the fact the these type of mortgage calculators not only help them capture prospects but convert them into 'interested and motivated' mortgage applicants indicating an awareness of the consumer and marketing uses of these calculators and their material impact. While opinions may differ as to what is material, federal regulators have described generally when a representation, omission, act or practice maybe considered material. "A material misrepresentation is one that is likely to affect a consumer's choice or conduct concerning a product or service. Consumer injury is likely if inaccurate information about costs, benefits, or significant limitations related to the product or service would be material."

As a consequence of using Rent v. Buy and Save In Tax mortgage calculators, unsuspecting consumers are likely being led into mortgage transactions expecting to enjoy mortgage related tax savings that won't occur and/or believing that a mortgage is a tax wise step, while not being made aware of the tax benefit of a (optimal) mortgage or a mortgage free home. Someone making a rent versus buy decision, counting on the overstated tax benefit of the mortgage interest deduction, could be misled from the outset. This wrong signal could result in financial harm to consumers. It's important to note that a worthwhile and informative disclosure does not need to be lengthy, for example: (1) It is only to the extent that this calculated value exceeds the standard deduction for your tax filing status that you may see benefit from the MID. (2) Please note that a mortgage free home could also have tax benefits. Please consult your tax or financial professional.

Banks on and through their websites have consistently omitted imputed rent as a value in their analysis, examinations and evaluations of the value of the mortgage interest deduction, thus, failing to present a balanced picture when comparing renting a home to owning a home and the related tax values and benefits.

Part Six: Conclusion

The results of this study identify the individual banks reviewed in the largest Metropolitan Statistical Area (MSA) for every state in the union and documents not only their individual market share, but the fact that collectively they have 88.80% of all FDIC insured bank deposits throughout the entire United States and while only 21% of the banks reviewed (1 in 5) made defective Rent v. Buy and Save in Tax mortgage calculators available on or through their websites, these FDIC insured banking institutions tend to have the largest market shares as they account for more than 64% of all FDIC insured bank deposits.

The Report goes on to identify the principal factors regulators look for in the determination of predatory, unfair and/or a deceptive act or practices and provides a link to Rent v. Buy mortgage calculators made available online by FDIC insured bank in the largest Metropolitan Statistical Areas throughout the USA. The Report identifies and enumerates a number of material representations, omissions, acts and practices from the perspective of a reasonable (but informed) consumer that are likely to be found misleading, deceptive, a cause of substantial consumer injuries and to affect a consumer's choice and/or conduct in relation to a decision to rent, buy and/or finance a principal residence.

The findings indicate that: 1) There is a lack of objective mortgage financial advice in the marketplace; 2) Rent v Buy and Save in Tax mortgage calculators aren't always what they appear to be; 3) There's a financially unhealthy institutionalized financial bias[xxxvii] that favors the mortgage interest deduction; 4) There is a tendency by even the best scholars[xxxviii] to focus on and promote the mortgage interest deduction to the exclusion of less costly and readily available benefits; 5) Individual consumers have a difficult time identifying credible, competent, objective mortgage advisory tools and services; 6) HUD, the Federal Reserve, FDIC and other federal and state banking regulators implicitly have trouble distinguishing between marketing material and tools and objective financial educational information and tools; 7) Mainstream FDIC insured banks and others not only have the capacity and ability to engage in predatory lending practices, they now have a retraceable history of either wittingly or unwittingly doing so; 8) Internet and the most sophisticated financially bank savvy consumers and regulators have implicitly been unable to detect this (now historical) practice; 9) the Department of Justice and the Federal Trade Commission utilize the Herfendahl-Hirschman Index of market concentration as a tool to measure predatory (anti-competitive) practices (likely to create or enhance market power or facilitate its exercise); and 10) The results of this study indicate that the provision of defective Rent v. Buy mortgage calculators is highly concentrated in the largest MSA in every state as the HHI rose on average 3,117 points, more than 30X the traditional guideline number for moderately concentrated markets and more than 60X the guideline number for highly concentrated markets.

The findings demonstratively illustrate that it's not only the un-banked, minorities, the credit challenged, the financially unsophisticated, but the well banked, internet savvy and financially sophisticated who are capable of being and are in fact being subjected to what a reasonable person could conclude is predatory, unfair and/or deceptive mortgage practices.

APPENDIX A

Appendix A:

TABLE 1

1	State:	Alabama
	Metropolitan Area:	Birmingham - Hoover

Rank		Institution Name	Market Share	Rent v. Buy (RvB) Calculator	FDIC Certificate #	Calculator Performance	Actual HHI Points
1		AMSOUTH	17.44%	Yes	26800		304.1536
2		WACHOVIA BANK NATIONAL ASSN	15.15%	No	33869		229.5225
3		COMPASS BANK	12.70%	Yes	19048		161.2900
4		REGIONS BANK	11.90%	Yes	12368		141.6100
5		FIRST COMMERCIAL BANK	6.13%	No	26359		37.5769
6		NEW SOUTH FSB	5.43%	Yes	32276		29.4849
7		COLONIAL BANK NATIONAL ASSN	4.40%	No	9609		19.3600
8		FIRST AMERICAN BANK	4.17%	No	23577		17.3889
9		NEXITY BANK	2.80%	No	19794		7.8400
10		SUPERIOR BANK	2.18%	No	17750		4.7524
11		FIRST NB OF JASPER	1.93%	No	2808		3.7249
12		SERVIFIRST BANK	1.57%	No	57993		2.4649
13		METRO BANK	1.50%	No	27510		2.2500
14		CAPITALSOUTH BANK	1.26%	No	22130		1.5876
	A	Total Market Share of Banks Reviewed	**88.56%**	**14**	Banks Actual HHI Points		963.0066
	B	MSA Mean Market Share Per Bank Reviewed	**6.33%**		RvB Actual HHI Points		636.5385
	C	MSA Median Market Share Per Bank Reviewed	**4.29%**				
	D	Market Share of Banks with Rent v. Buy Calculator	47.47%	**4**	RvB Pro Forma HHI Points		2253.4009
	E	MSA Mean Market Share Per RvB Bank	11.87%				
	F	MSA Median Market Share Per RvB Bank	12.30%		Leon L. Morris ©		

Legend	
Top 50 National Bank	
Market Share of Bank Reviewed	
Bank w. Rent v. Buy Calculator	
Calculator Performed Correctly	
Calculator Performed Incorrectly	
HHI Points	
Save in Taxes – Calculator	ST
No retail Mortgage loans solicited	NRML

Birmingham MSA

Herfendahl-Herschman	**Index**	# of Institutions
Actual	969.6851	44
Pro-Forma	2586.046	41
Change > 100	**1616.3609**	

TABLE 2

Rank	2	State:	Alaska				
		Metropolitan Area:	Anchorage				
Rank		Institution Name	Market Share	Rent v. Buy (RvB) Calculator	FDIC Certificate #	Calculator Performance	Actual HHI Points
1		WELLS FARGO BANK NA	40.88%	Yes	3511		1671.1744
2		FIRST NATIONAL BANK ALASKA	25.77%	No	16130		664.0929
3		NORTHRIM BANK	19.57%	Yes	33216		382.9849
4		KEYBANK	12.47%	Yes	17534		155.5009
5		ALASKA FIRST B&T NA	1.30%	No	27311		1.6900
	A	Market (Mkt.) Share of Banks Reviewed	**99.99%**	**5**	Banks reviewed HHI Points		2875.4431
	B	MSA Mean Market Share Per Bank Reviewed	**20.00%**		RvB Actual HHI Points		2209.6602
	C	MSA Median Market Share Per Bank Reviewed	**19.57%**				
	D	Mkt. Share of Banks with Rent v. Buy calculator	72.92%	**3**	RvB Pro Forma HHI Points		5317.3264
	E	MSA Mean Market Share Per RvB Bank	24.31%				
	F	MSA Median Market Share for RvB Banks	19.57%		Leon L. Morris ©		

Legend	
Top 50 National Bank	
Market Share of Bank Reviewed	
Bank w. Rent v. Buy Calculator	
Calculator Performed Correctly	
Calculator Performed Incorrectly	
HHI Points	
Save in Taxes – Calculator	ST
No retail Mortgage loans solicited	NRML

Entire Anchorage MSA

Herfendahl-Herschman	Index	# of Institutions
Actual	2875.8136	5
Pro-Forma	5983.8658	3
Change > 100	**3108.0522**	

TABLE 3

3	State	Arizona
	Metropolitan Area	PHOENIX-MESA-SCOTTSDALE, AZ

Rank		Institution Name	Market Share	Rent v. Buy (RvB) Calculator	FDIC Certificate #	Calculator Performance	Actual HHI Points
1		JP MORGAN CHASE BANK NA	25.60%	Yes	628		655.3600
2		BANK OF AMERICA NA	20.52%	Yes	3510		421.0704
3		WELLS FARGO BANK NA	18.94%	Yes	3511		358.7236
4		M&I MARSHALL & ILSEY BANK	4.05%	Yes	1020		16.4025
5		COMPASS BANK	3.43%	Yes	19048		11.7649
6		WORLD SAVINGS BANK FSB	3.41%	No	27076		11.6281
7		FIRST NB OF ARIZONA	2.75%	No	27508		7.5625
8	ST	NATIONAL BANK OF ARIZONA	2.74%	Yes	20626		7.5076
9		MERIDIAN BANK NATIONAL ASSN	2.51%	No	22644		6.3001
10		OHIO SAVINGS BANK FSB	2.14%	Yes	29776		4.5796
11		WASHINGTON MUTUAL BANK	1.84%	Yes	32633		3.3856
12	ST	NORTHERN TRUST BANK NA	1.19%	Yes	24743		1.4161
	A	Market Share of Banks Reviewed	**89.12%**	**12**	Banks reviewed HHI Points		1505.7010
	B	MSA Mean Market Share Per Bank Reviewed	**7.43%**		RvB Actual HHI Points		1480.2103
	C	MSA Median Market Share Per Bank Reviewed	**3.08%**				
	D	Market Share of Banks with Rent v. Buy calculator	80.45%	9	RvB Pro Forma HHI Points		6472.2025
	E	MSA Mean Market Share Per RvB Bank	8.94%				
	F	MSA Median Market Share for RvB Banks	3.43%		Leon L. Morris ©		

Legend	
Top 50 National Bank	
Market Share of Bank Reviewed	
Bank w. Rent v. Buy Calculator	
Calculator Performed Correctly	
Calculator Performed Incorrectly	
HHI Points	
Save in Taxes - Calculator	ST
No retail Mortgage loans solicited	NRML

Phoenix		
Herfendahl-Herschman	**Index**	# of Institutions
Actual	1509.8192	67
Pro-Forma	6501.2434	59
Change > 100	**4991.4242**	

TABLE 4

4	State	Arkansas
	Metropolitan Area	Little Rock - North Little Rock

Rank		Institution Name	Market Share	Rent v. Buy (RvB) Calculator	FDIC Certificate #	Calculator Performance	Actual HHI Points
1		REGIONS BANK	16.31%	Yes	12368		266.0161
2		BANK OF AMERICA NA	13.83%	Yes	3510		191.2689
3	ST	METROPOLITAN NATIONAL BANK	10.28%	Yes	20280		105.6784
4		BANK OF THE OZARKS	9.28%	Yes	110		86.1184
5		ARVEST BANK	5.23%	No	8728		27.3529
6		TWIN CITY BANK	4.60%	Yes	33472		21.1600
7		U S BANK NATIONAL ASSN	4.50%	Yes	6548		20.2500
8		FIRST STATE BANK	3.64%	No	11241		13.2496
9		PULASKI BANK & TRUST CO	3.34%	No	17562		11.1556
10		FIRST SECURITY BK OF CONWAY	2.92%	Yes	33502		8.5264
11		ONE BANK & TRUST NATIONAL ASSN	2.43%	No	17800		5.9049
12		COMMUNITY BANK	2.19%	Yes	1749		4.7961
13		FIRST ARKANSAS BANK & TRUST	2.01%	Yes	16849		4.0401
14		UNION BANK OF BENTON	1.71%	No	17322		2.9241
15		BANCORPSOUTH BANK	1.41%	No	11813		1.9881
16		ARKANSAS BANKERS BANK	1.38%	No Retail Mortgages	32960		1.9044
17		BANK OF ENGLAND	1.38%	No	13303		1.9044
18		SIMMONS FIRST NATIONAL BANK	1.35%	Yes	3890		1.8225
19		NATIONAL BK AR N LITTLE ROCK	1.27%	Yes	23331		1.6129
20		FIRST STATE BANK	1.11%	Yes	15050		1.2321
21		BANK OF LITTLE ROCK	1.08%	Yes	91280		1.1664
22		CAPITAL BANK	1.03%	No	34562		1.0609
23		FIRST SECURITY BANK	1.02%	Yes	5633		1.0404
	A	Market Share of Banks Reviewed	**93.30%**	**23**	Banks reviewed HHI Points		782.1736
	B	MSA Mean Market Share Per Bank Reviewed	**4.06%**		RvB Actual HHI Points		714.7287
	C	MSA Median Market Share Per Bank Reviewed	**2.19%**				
	D	Market Share of Banks with Rent v. Buy calculator	71.75%	**14**	RvB Pro Forma HHI Points		5148.0625
	E	MSA Mean Market Share Per RvB Bank	5.13%				
	F	MSA Median Market Share for RvB Banks	2.56%		Leon L. Morris ©		

Entire Little Rock MSA		
Herfendahl-Herschman	**Index**	# of Institutions
Actual	786.8591	37
Pro-Forma	5218.3367	24
Change > 100	**4431.4776**	

Legend	
Top 50 National Bank	(yellow)
Market Share of Bank Reviewed	(green)
Bank w. Rent v. Buy Calculator	(orange)
Calculator Performed Correctly	(light green)
Calculator Performed Incorrectly	(red)
HHI Points	(blue)
Save in Taxes - Calculator	ST
No retail Mortgage loans solicited	NRML

TABLE 5

5	State	California
	Metropolitan Area	Los Angeles- Long Beach - Santa Ana

Rank		Institution Name	Market Share	Rent v. Buy (RvB) Calculator	FDIC Certificate #	Calculator Performance	Actual HHI Points
1		BANK OF AMERICA NA	18.93%	Yes	3510		358.3449
2		WASHINGTON MUTUAL BANK	11.52%	Yes	32633		132.7104
3		WELLS FARGO BANK NA	10.89%	Yes	3511		118.5921
4		UNION BANK OF CALIFORNIA NA	5.78%	Yes	22826		33.4084
5		CITIBANK WEST FSB	4.30%	Statement	57443		18.4900
6		CITY NATIONAL BANK	3.44%	No	17281		11.8336
7		INDYMAC BANK FSB	3.21%	Yes	29730		10.3041
8		WORLD SAVINGS BANK FSB	3.20%	No	27076		10.2400
9	ST	BANK OF THE WEST	2.85%	Yes	3514		8.1225
10		FREMONT INVESTMENT & LOAN	2.59%	NRML	25653		6.7081
11	ST	DOWNEY SAVINGS & LOAN ASSN FA	2.26%	Yes	30968		5.1076
12		EAST WEST BANK	2.23%	No	31628		4.9729
13		COMERICA BANK	2.12%	No	983		4.4944
14		FIRST FED BK OF CA A FSB	1.92%	No	28536		3.6864
15		CALIFORNIA NATIONAL BANK	1.53%	No	34659		2.3409
16		CATHY BANK	1.37%	No	18503		1.8769
17		CALIFORNIA BANK & TRUST	1.21%	Yes	20852		1.4641
	A	Market Share of Banks Reviewed	**79.35%**	17	Banks reviewed HHI Points		732.6973
	B	MSA Mean Market Share Per Bank Reviewed	**4.67%**		RvB Actual HHI Points		668.0541
	C	MSA Median Market Share Per Bank Reviewed	**2.85%**				
	D	Market Share of Banks with Rent v. Buy calculator	56.65%	8	RvB Pro Forma HHI Points		3209.2225
	E	MSA Mean Market Share Per RvB Bank	7.08%				
	F	MSA Median Market Share for RvB Banks	4.50%		Leon L. Morris ©		

Legend	
Top 50 National Bank	(yellow)
Market Share of Bank Reviewed	(green)
Bank w. Rent v. Buy Calculator	(orange)
Calculator Performed Correctly	(light green)
Calculator Performed Incorrectly	(red)
HHI Points	(blue)
Save in Taxes - Calculator	ST
No retail Mortgage loans solicited	NRML

Entire Los Angeles MSA

Herfendahl-Herschman	Index	# of Institutions
Actual	741.8627	164
Pro-Forma	3283.8785	157
Change > 100	**2542.0158**	

TABLE 6

6	State	Colorado
	Metropolitan Area	Denver- Aurora

Rank		Institution Name	Market Share	Rent v. Buy (RvB) Calculator	FDIC Certificate #	Calculator Performance	Actual HHI Points
1		WELLS FARGO BANK NA	19.98%	Yes	3511		399.2000
2		U S BANK NATIONAL ASSN	11.37%	Yes	6548		129.2769
3		WORLD SAVINGS BANK FSB	7.37%	No	27076		54.3169
4		JP MORGAN CHASE BANK NA	5.14%	Yes	628		26.4196
5		FISERV TRUST CO	5.01%	NRML	91322		25.1001
6		KEYBANK NATIONAL ASSN	5.00%	Yes	17534		25.0000
7	ST	BANK OF THE WEST	4.67%	Yes	3514		21.8089
8		MATRIX CAPITAL BANK *United Western Bank	3.27%	NRML	31293		10.6929
9		GUARANTY BANK & TRUST CO	2.82%	No	17482		7.9524
10		COBIZ BANK NATIONAL ASSN	2.24%	No	22683		5.0176
11	ST	VECTRA BANK COLORADO NA	2.03%	Yes	2993		4.1209
12		FIRST BANK OF COLORADO	1.92%	No	18714		3.6864
13		CITYWIDE BANKS	1.76%	No	19858		3.0976
14		COLORADO STATE B & T NA	1.60%	No	1769		2.5600
15		COMPASS BANK	1.42%	Yes	19048		2.0164
16		TCF NATIONAL BANK	1.14%	No	28330		1.2996
17		FIRST BANK OF SOUTH JEFF CO	1.09%	No	22613		1.1881
	A	Market Share of Banks Reviewed	**77.83%**	**17**	Banks reviewed HHI Points		722.7543
	B	MSA Mean Market Share Per Bank Reviewed	**4.58%**		RvB Actual HHI Points		607.8427
	C	MSA Median Market Share Per Bank Reviewed	**2.82%**				
	D	Market Share of Banks with Rent v. Buy calculator	49.61%	7	RvB Pro Forma HHI Points		2461.1521
	E	MSA Mean Market Share Per RvB Bank	7.09%				
	F	MSA Median Market Share for RvB Banks	5.00%		Leon L. Morris ©		

*Matrix Capital changed it's name to United Western Bank on September 7, 2006.

Legend	
Top 50 National Bank	
Market Share of Bank Reviewed	
Bank w. Rent v. Buy Calculator	
Calculator Performed Correctly	
Calculator Performed Incorrectly	
HHI Points	
Save in Taxes - Calculator	ST
No retail Mortgage loans solicited	NRML

Denver		
Herfendahl-Herschman	**Index**	# of Institutions
Actual	734.7589	86
Pro-Forma	3318.4899	79
Change > 100	**2583.7310**	

TABLE 7

7	State	Connecticut
	Metropolitan Area	Bridgeport - Stanford - Norwalk, CT

Rank		Institution Name	Market Share	Rent v. Buy (RvB) Calculator	FDIC Certificate #	Calculator Performance	Actual HHI Points
1	ST	PEOPLES BANK	21.78%	Yes	27334		474.3684
2		WACHOVIA BANK NATIONAL ASSN	15.32%	No	33869		234.7024
3		JP MORGAN CHASE BANK NA	12.08%	Yes	628		145.9264
4		BANK OF AMERICA NA	11.24%	Yes	3510		126.3376
5		CITIBANK FSB	5.52%	Statement	28251		30.4704
6		WEBSTER BANK NATIONAL ASSN	5.04%	Yes	18221		25.4016
7		FAIRFIELD COUNTYBANK CORP	4.37%	Yes	18213		19.0969
8		UNION SAVINGS BANK	3.84%	Yes	18190		14.7456
9		FIRST COUNTY BANK	3.31%	Yes	18204		10.9561
10		TD BANKNORTH NATIONAL ASSN	2.68%	Yes	18409		7.1824
11		PATRIOT NATIONAL BANK	2.02%	No	33928		4.0804
12		BANK OF NEW YORK	1.98%	Yes	639		3.9204
13		NEWTON SAVINGS BANK	1.88%	Yes	18199		3.5344
14		SAVINGS BANK OF DANBURY	1.64%	No	15912		2.6896
15		NEWMIL BANK now Webster Bank 10/06	1.21%	Yes	18259		1.4641
16		CONNECTICUT CMTY BANK NA	1.19%	No	34876		1.4161
	A	Market Share of Banks Reviewed	**95.10%**	16	Banks reviewed HHI Points		1106.2928
	B	MSA Mean Market Share Per Bank Reviewed	**5.94%**		RvB Actual HHI Points		832.9339
	C	MSA Median Market Share Per Bank Reviewed	**3.58%**				
	D	Market Share of Banks with Rent v. Buy calculator	69.41%	11	RvB Pro Forma HHI Points		**4817.7481**
	E	MSA Mean Market Share Per RvB Bank	6.31%				
	F	MSA Median Market Share for RvB Banks	3.84%		Leon L. Morris ©		

Legend	
Top 50 National Bank	
Market Share of Bank Reviewed	
Bank w. Rent v. Buy Calculator	
Calculator Performed Correctly	
Calculator Performed Incorrectly	
HHI Points	
Save in Taxes - Calculator	ST
No retail Mortgage loans solicited	NRML

Entire Bridgeport MSA

Herfendahl-Herschman	Index	# of Institutions
Actual	1109.3498	30
Pro-Forma	5095.1143	20
Change > 100	**3985.7645**	

TABLE 8

8	State	Delaware
	Metropolitan Area	Wilmington

Rank		Institution Name	Market Share	Rent v. Buy (RvB) Calculator	FDIC Certificate #	Calculator Performance	Actual HHI Points
1		ING BANK FSB	30.17%	**No**	35489		910.2289
2		CHASE BANK USA NATIONAL ASSN	17.61%	Yes	23702		310.1121
3		FIA CARD SERVICES NA Bank of America	17.25%	Yes	33318		297.5625
4		LEHMAN BROTHERS BANK FSB	10.64%	**No**	30890		113.2096
5		DISCOVER BANK	8.74%	**No**	5649		76.3876
6	ST	WILMINGTON TRUST CO	4.96%	Yes	680		24.6016
7		PNC BANK DELAWARE	1.53%	Comments	679		2.3409
8		CITIBANK DELAWARE	1.38%	Statement	24029		1.9044
9		CITICORP TRUST BANK FSB	1.19%	**No**	18708		1.4161
10		WACHOVIA BANK OF DELAWARE NA	1.19%	**No**	33931		1.4161
11		WILMINGTON SVG FUND SOCIETY	1.03%	**No**	17838		1.0609
	A	Market Share of Banks Reviewed	**95.69%**	11	Banks reviewed HHI Points		1740.2407
	B	MSA Mean Market Share Per Bank Reviewed	**8.70%**		RvB Actual HHI Points		632.2762
	C	MSA Median Market Share Per Bank Reviewed	**4.96%**				
	D	Market Share of Banks with Rent v. Buy calculator	39.82%	3	RvB Pro Forma HHI Points		1585.6324
	E	MSA Mean Market Share Per RvB Bank	13.27%				
	F	MSA Median Market Share for RvB Banks	17.25%		Leon L. Morris ©		

Legend	
Top 50 National Bank	
Market Share of Bank Reviewed	
Bank w. Rent v. Buy Calculator	
Calculator Performed Correctly	
Calculator Performed Incorrectly	
HHI Points	
Save in Taxes - Calculator	ST
No retail Mortgage loans solicited	NRML

Wilmington		
Herfendahl-Herschman	**Index**	# of Institutions
Actual	1741.9743	43
Pro-Forma	2695.3203	41
Change > 100	**953.3460**	

TABLE 9

9	State	Florida
	Metropolitan Area	Jacksonville

Rank		Institution Name	Market Share	Rent v. Buy (RvB) Calculator	FDIC Certificate #	Calculator Performance	Actual HHI Points
1		BANK OF AMERICA NA	32.83%	Yes	3510		1077.8089
2		WACHOVIA BANK NATIONAL ASSN	25.40%	**No**	33869		645.1600
3		EVERBANK	10.88%	Yes	34775		118.3744
4	ST	SUNTRUST BANK	6.78%	Yes	867		45.9684
5		COMPASS BANK	4.66%	Yes	19048		21.7156
6		AMSOUTH BANK	2.24%	Yes	26800		5.0176
7		MERCANTILE BANK	1.64%	Yes	27515		2.6896
8		PROPSERITY BANK	1.53%	Yes	24963		2.3409
9		R-G CROWN BANK	1.37%	**No**	32337		1.8760
10		BRANCH BANKING & TRUST CO	1.19%	Yes	9846		1.4161
11		FIRST GUARANTY B&T CO.	1.16%	No	16579		1.3456
12		ATLANTIC COAST BANK	1.08%	**No**	45826		1.1664
	A	Market Share of Banks Reviewed	**90.76%**	12	Banks reviewed HHI Points		1924.8795
	B	MSA Mean Market Share Per Bank Reviewed	**7.56%**		RvB Actual HHI Points		1275.3315
	C	MSA Median Market Share Per Bank Reviewed	**1.94%**				
	D	Market Share of Banks with Rent v. Buy calculator	61.75%	8	RvB Pro Forma HHI Points		**3813.0625**
	E	MSA Mean Market Share Per RvB Bank	7.72%				
	F	MSA Median Market Share for RvB Banks	3.45%		Leon L. Morris ©		

Legend	
Top 50 National Bank	
Market Share of Bank Reviewed	
Bank w. Rent v. Buy Calculator	
Calculator Performed Correctly	
Calculator Performed Incorrectly	
HHI Points	
Save in Taxes - Calculator	ST
No retail Mortgage loans solicited	NRML

Entire Jacksonville MSA

Herfendahl-Herschman	Index	# of Institutions
Actual	1929.4173	38
Pro-Forma	4468.2371	31
Change > 100	**2538.8198**	

TABLE 10

10	State	Georgia
	Metropolitan Area	Atlanta

Rank		Institution Name	Market Share	Rent v. Buy (RvB) Calculator	FDIC Certificate #	Calculator Performance	Actual HHI Points
1		SUNTRUST BANK	29.06%	Yes	867		844.4836
2		WACHOVIA BANK NATIONAL ASSN	19.37%	No	33869		375.1969
3		BANK OF AMERICA NA	12.28%	Yes	3510		150.7984
4		BRANCH BANKING & TRUST CO	2.91%	Yes	9846		8.4681
5		BANK OF NORTH GEORGIA	2.78%	No	31203		7.7284
6	ST	NETBANK	2.49%	Yes	32575		6.2001
7	ST	REGIONS BANK	2.28%	Yes	12368		5.1984
8		MAINSTREET BANK now BB&T	1.43%	Yes	9243		2.0449
9		FIDELITY BANK	1.15%	No	21440		1.3225
10		GEORGIAN BANK	1.09%	No	57151		1.1881
11		UNITED COMMUNITY BANK	1%	Yes	16889		1.0000
	A	Market Share of Banks Reviewed	**75.84%**	11	Banks reviewed HHI Points		1403.6294
	B	MSA Mean Market Share Per Bank Reviewed	**6.89%**		RvB Actual HHI Points		1018.1935
	C	MSA Median Market Share Per Bank Reviewed	**2.49%**				
	D	Market Share of Banks with Rent v. Buy calculator	51.45%	7	RvB Pro Forma HHI Points		**2647.1025**
	E	MSA Mean Market Share Per RvB Bank	7.35%				
	F	MSA Median Market Share for RvB Banks	2.49%		Leon L. Morris ©		

Legend	
Top 50 National Bank	
Market Share of Bank Reviewed	
Bank w. Rent v. Buy Calculator	
Calculator Performed Correctly	
Calculator Performed Incorrectly	
HHI Points	
Save in Taxes - Calculator	ST
No retail Mortgage loans solicited	NRML

Atlanta

Herfendahl-Herschman	**Index**	# of Institutions
Actual	1411.9399	152
Pro-Forma	3040.9748	146
Change > 100	**1629.0349**	

TABLE 11

11	State	Hawaii
	Metropolitan Area	Honolulu

Rank		Institution Name	Market Share	Rent v. Buy (RvB) Calculator	FDIC Certificate #	Calculator Performance	Actual HHI Points
1		FIRST HAWAIIAN BANK	30.27%	Yes	17985		916.2729
2	ST	BANK OF HAWAII	26.77%	Yes	18053		716.6329
3		AMERICAN SAVINGS BANK FSB	18.06%	Yes	32526		506.7636
4		CENTRAL PACIFIC BANK	15.76%	Yes	17308		248.3776
5		TERRITORIAL SAVINGS BANK	4.09%	Yes	30836		16.7281
6		FINANCE FACTORS LTD	2.05%	Yes	25158		4.2025
7		HAWAII NATIONAL BANK	1.73%	**No**	18296		2.9929
	A	Market Share of Banks Reviewed	**98.73%**	7	Banks reviewed HHI Points		2411.9705
	B	MSA Mean Market Share Per Bank Reviewed	**14.10%**		RvB Actual HHI Points		2408.9776
	C	MSA Median Market Share Per Bank Reviewed	**15.76%**				
	D	Market Share of Banks with Rent v. Buy calculator	97.00%	6	RvB Pro Forma HHI Points		**9409.0000**
	E	MSA Mean Market Share Per RvB Bank	16.17%				
	F	MSA Median Market Share for RvB Banks	16.91%		Leon L. Morris ©		

Legend	
Top 50 National Bank	
Market Share of Bank Reviewed	
Bank w. Rent v. Buy Calculator	
Calculator Performed Correctly	
Calculator Performed Incorrectly	
HHI Points	
Save in Taxes - Calculator	ST
No retail Mortgage loans solicited	NRML

Entire Honolulu MSA

Herfendahl-Herschman	Index	# of Institutions
Actual	2411.9706	12
Pro-Forma	9412.7572	7
Change > 100	**7000.7866**	

TABLE 12

12	State	Idaho
	Metropolitan Area	Boise City - Nampa, ID

Rank		Institution Name	Market Share	Rent v. Buy (RvB) Calculator	FDIC Certificate #	Calculator Performance	Actual HHI Points
1		U S BANK NATIONAL ASSN	24.44%	Yes	6548		597.3136
2		WELLS FARGO BANK NA	19.60%	Yes	3511		384.1600
3		KEYBANK NATIONAL ASSN	8.30%	Yes	17534		68.8900
4		BANK OF THE CASCADES	6.14%	**No**	22407		37.6996
5		HOME FEDERAL BANK	5.78%	**No**	28258		33.4084
6		WASHINGTON FS&LA	5.24%	**No**	28088		27.4576
7		BANK OF AMERICA NA	4.95%	Yes	3510		24.5025
8		IDAHO INDEPENDENT BANK	4.26%	**No**	33845		18.1476
9		WASHINGTON TRUST BANK	3.81%	Yes	1281		14.5161
10		WASHINGTON MUTUAL BANK FSB	2.61%	Yes	33891		6.8121
11		WASHINGTON MUTUAL BANK	2.59%	Yes	32633		6.7081
12		IDAHO BANKING CO	2.43%	Yes	34317		5.9049
13	ST	D L EVANS BANK	2.14%	**No**	11666		4.5796
14		MOUNTAIN WEST BANK	1.99%	**No**	33844		3.9601
15		SYRINGA BANK	1.93%	**No**	34296		3.7249
16	ST	ZIONS FIRST NATIONAL BANK	1.07%	Yes	2270		1.1449
	A	Market Share of Banks Reviewed	**97.28%**	16	Banks reviewed HHI Points		1238.9300
	B	MSA Mean Market Share Per Bank Reviewed	**6.08%**		RvB Actual HHI Points		1109.9522
	C	MSA Median Market Share Per Bank Reviewed	**4.04%**				
	D	Market Share of Banks with Rent v. Buy calculator	69.80%	9	RvB Pro Forma HHI Points		**4872.0400**
	E	MSA Mean Market Share Per RvB Bank	7.76%				
	F	MSA Median Market Share for RvB Banks	3.81%		Leon L. Morris ©		

Legend	
Top 50 National Bank	
Market Share of Bank Reviewed	
Bank w. Rent v. Buy Calculator	
Calculator Performed Correctly	
Calculator Performed Incorrectly	
HHI Points	
Save in Taxes - Calculator	ST
No retail Mortgage loans solicited	NRML

Entire Boise MSA

Herfendahl-Herschman	Index	# of Institutions
Actual	1240.9446	21
Pro-Forma	5004.8252	13
Change > 100	**3763.8806**	

TABLE 13

13	State	Illinois
	Metropolitan Area	Chicago-Naperville - Joliet, IL-IN-WI

Rank		Institution Name	Market Share	Rent v. Buy (RvB) Calculator	FDIC Certificate #	Calculator Performance	Actual HHI Points
1		JP MORGAN CHASE BANK NA	15.30%	Yes	628		234.0900
2	ST	LASALLE BANK NATIONAL ASSN	14.11%	Yes	15407		199.0921
3	ST	HARRIS NATIONAL ASSN	9.53%	Yes	16571		90.8209
4	ST	FIFTH THIRD BANK	3.23%	Yes	993		10.4329
5		CORUS BANK NATIONAL ASSN	3.18%	NRML	13693		10.1124
6	ST	CHARTER ONE BANK NA	2.79%	Yes	28932		7.7841
7	ST	NORTHERN TRUST CO	2.79%	Yes	913		7.7841
8		CITIBANK FSB	2.57%	Statement	28251		6.6049
9		MID AMERICA BANK FSB	2.18%	Yes	28671		4.7524
10		FIRST MIDWEST BANK	2.15%	**No**	3709		4.6225
11		BANK OF AMERICA NA	1.81%	Yes	3510		3.2761
12		NATIONAL CITY BANK OF THE MW	1.78%	Yes	5029		3.1684
13		MB FINANCIAL BANK NA	1.54%	Yes	3628		2.3716
14		TCF NATIONAL BANK	1.14%	**No**	28330		1.2996
15		PARK NATIONAL BANK	1.12%	**No**	11677		1.2544
16		COLE TAYLOR BANK	1.03%	No	22599		1.0609
	A	Market Share of Banks Reviewed	**66.25%**	16	Banks reviewed HHI Points		588.5273
	B	MSA Mean Market Share Per Bank Reviewed	**4.14%**		RvB Actual HHI Points		563.5726
	C	MSA Median Market Share Per Bank Reviewed	**2.38%**				
	D	Market Share of Banks with Rent v. Buy calculator	55.06%	10	RvB Pro Forma HHI Points		**3031.6036**
	E	MSA Mean Market Share Per RvB Bank	5.51%				
	F	MSA Median Market Share for RvB Banks	2.79%		Leon L. Morris ©		

Legend	
Top 50 National Bank	
Market Share of Bank Reviewed	
Bank w. Rent v. Buy Calculator	
Calculator Performed Correctly	
Calculator Performed Incorrectly	
HHI Points	
Save in Taxes - Calculator	ST
No retail Mortgage loans solicited	NRML

Entire Chicago MSA		
Herfendahl-Herschman	**Index**	# of Institutions
Actual	599.0443	305
Pro-Forma	3065.2984	296
Change > 100	**2466.2541**	

TABLE 14

14	State	Indiana
	Metropolitan Area	Indianapolis

Rank		Institution Name	Market Share	Rent v. Buy (RvB) Calculator	FDIC Certificate #	Calculator Performance	Actual HHI Points
1		JP MORGAN CHASE BANK NA	23.01%	Yes	628		529.4601
2		NATIONAL CITY BANK OF IN	18.39%	Yes	4347		338.1921
3	ST	FIFTH THIRD BANK	9.50%	Yes	993		90.2500
4		UNION FED BK IF INPOLIS acquired by SKY	8.01%	Yes	32614		64.1601
5		FIRST INDIANA BANK NA	6.02%	No	29057		36.2404
6		KEYBANK NATIONAL ASSN	3.65%	Yes	17534		13.3225
7		REGIONS BANK	3.55%	Yes	12368		12.6025
8		NATIONAL BANK OF INPOLIS	3.08%	No	33860		9.4864
9		HUNTINGTON NATIONAL BANK	2.46%	Yes	6560		6.0516
10		LINCOLN BANK*	2.10%	Yes	28617		4.4100
11	ST	CHARTER ONE BANK NA	1.94%	Yes	28932		3.7636
12	ST	OLD NATIONAL BANK	1.68%	Yes	3832		2.8224
13		FIRST INTERNET BANK OF IN	1.38%	Yes	34607		1.9044
14		IRWIN UNION BANK & TRUST CO	1.23%	No	10100		1.5129
15		FIRST NATIONAL BANK & TRUST	1.21%	No	16298		1.4641
16		FLAGSTAR BANK FSB	1.13%	Yes	32541		1.2769
	A	Market Share of Banks Reviewed	**88.34%**	16	Banks reviewed HHI Points		1116.9200
	B	MSA Mean Market Share Per Bank Reviewed	**5.52%**		RvB Actual HHI Points		1068.2162
	C	MSA Median Market Share Per Bank Reviewed	**2.77%**				
	D	Market Share of Banks with Rent v. Buy calculator	76.80%	12	RvB Pro Forma HHI Points		**5898.2400**
	E	MSA Mean Market Share Per RvB Bank	6.40%				
	F	MSA Median Market Share for RvB Banks	3.01%		Leon L. Morris ©		

Legend	
Top 50 National Bank	
Market Share of Bank Reviewed	
Bank w. Rent v. Buy Calculator	
Calculator Performed Correctly	
Calculator Performed Incorrectly	
HHI Points	
Save in Taxes - Calculator	ST
No retail Mortgage loans solicited	NRML

Entire Indianapolis MSA

Herfendahl-Herschman	Index	# of Institutions
Actual	1123.658	56
Pro-Forma	5957.2603	45
Change > 100	**4833.6023**	

TABLE 15

15	State	Iowa
	Metropolitan Area	Des Moines, IA

Rank		Institution Name	Market Share	Rent v. Buy (RvB) Calculator	FDIC Certificate #	Calculator Performance	Actual HHI Points
1		WELLS FARGO BANK NA	16.20%	Yes	3511		262.4400
2	ST	PRINCIPAL BANK	11.46%	Yes	34507		131.3316
3	ST	BANKERS TRUST CO NA	10.83%	Yes	953		117.2889
4		WEST BANK	9.17%	No	15614		84.0889
5		BANK OF AMERICA NA	6.91%	Yes	3510		47.7481
6		U S BANK NATIONAL ASSN	6.74%	Yes	6548		45.4276
7		COMMUNITY STB NA	3.93%	Yes	18272		15.4449
8		FIRST AMERICAN BANK	3.69%	Yes	14808		13.6161
9	ST	BANK OF THE WEST	3.50%	Yes	3514		12.2500
10		IOWA STATE BANK	2.11%	No	15808		4.4521
11		LIBERTY BANK FSB	1.81%	No	20594		3.2761
12		METABANK	1.70%	Yes	30776		2.8900
13		EARLHAM SAVINGS BANK	1.58%	No	5796		2.4964
14	ST	RACCOON VALLEY BANK	1.32%	Yes	245		1.7424
15		FIRST BANK	1.27%	No	4516		1.6129
16		POLK COUNTY BANK	1.18%	No	14194		1.3924
17		REGIONS BANK	1.11%	Yes	12368		1.2321
18		CITY STATE BANK	1.09%	Yes	14410		1.1881
	A	Market Share of Banks Reviewed	**85.60%**	18	Banks reviewed HHI Points		749.9186
	B	MSA Mean Market Share Per Bank Reviewed	**4.76%**		RvB Actual HHI Points		652.5998
	C	MSA Median Market Share Per Bank Reviewed	**3.60%**				
	D	Market Share of Banks with Rent v. Buy calculator	68.48%	12	RvB Pro Forma HHI Points		**4689.5104**
	E	MSA Mean Market Share Per RvB Bank	5.71%				
	F	MSA Median Market Share for RvB Banks	3.81%		Leon L. Morris ©		

Legend	
Top 50 National Bank	
Market Share of Bank Reviewed	
Bank w. Rent v. Buy Calculator	
Calculator Performed Correctly	
Calculator Performed Incorrectly	
HHI Points	
Save in Taxes - Calculator	ST
No retail Mortgage loans solicited	NRML

Des Moines

Herfendahl-Herschman	Index	# of Institutions
Actual	759.3428	53
Pro-Forma	4794.692	42
Change > 100	**4035.3492**	

TABLE 16

16	State	Kansas
	Metropolitan Area	Wichita

Rank		Institution Name	Market Share	Rent v. Buy (RvB) Calculator	FDIC Certificate #	Calculator Performance	Actual HHI Points
1	ST	INTRUST BANK NATIONAL ASSN	21.91%	Yes	4799		480.0481
2		BANK OF AMERICA NA	13.11%	Yes	3510		171.8721
3		FIDELITY BANK	10.44%	**No**	30895		108.9936
4		COMMERCE BANK NATIONAL ASN	7.41%	Yes	10911		54.9081
5		EMPRISE BANK	5.28%	Yes	4789		27.8784
6		WORLD SAVINGS BANK FSB	5.27%	No	27076		27.7729
7		CAPITOL FEDERAL SAVINGS BANK	4.64%	**No**	27981		21.5296
8		SOUTHWEST NATIONAL BANK	3.08%	**No**	4801		9.4864
9	ST	BANK OF THE WEST	2.92%	Yes	3514		8.5264
10		PRAIRIE STATE BANK now Emprise Bank	2.65%	Yes	12599		7.0225
11		LEGACY BANK	1.57%	**No**	17676		2.4649
12	ST	EQUITY BANK A NATIONAL ASSN	1.42%	Yes	25858		2.0164
13		ROSE HILL BANK	1.34%	**No**	13881		1.7956
14		FIRST BANK OF NEWTON	1.23%	**No**	4738		1.5129
15		MIDLAND NB OF NEWTON	1.20%	**No**	4739		1.4400
	A	Market Share of Banks Reviewed	**83.47%**	15	Banks reviewed HHI Points		927.2679
	B	MSA Mean Market Share Per Bank Reviewed	**5.56%**		RvB Actual HHI Points		752.2720
	C	MSA Median Market Share Per Bank Reviewed	**3.08%**				
	D	Market Share of Banks with Rent v. Buy calculator	54.70%	7	RvB Pro Forma HHI Points		**2992.0900**
	E	MSA Mean Market Share Per RvB Bank	7.81%				
	F	MSA Median Market Share for RvB Banks	5.28%		Leon L. Morris ©		

Legend	
Top 50 National Bank	
Market Share of Bank Reviewed	
Bank w. Rent v. Buy Calculator	
Calculator Performed Correctly	
Calculator Performed Incorrectly	
HHI Points	
Save in Taxes - Calculator	ST
No retail Mortgage loans solicited	NRML

Entire Wichita MSA		
Herfendahl-Herschman	**Index**	# of Institutions
Actual	936.2305	59
Pro-Forma	3175.5565	53
Change > 100	**2239.3260**	

TABLE 17

17	State	Kentucky
	Metropolitan Area	Lexington-Fayette, KY

Rank		Institution Name	Market Share	Rent v. Buy (RvB) Calculator	FDIC Certificate #	Calculator Performance	Actual HHI Points
1		JP MORGAN CHASE BANK NA	14.28%	Yes	628		203.9184
2	ST	FIFTH THIRD BANK	14.02%	Yes	993		196.5604
3		CENTRAL BANK & TRUST CO	13.94%	No	15815		194.3236
4		NATIONAL CITY BANK OF KY	7.34%	Yes	2756		53.8756
5		BRANCH BANKING & TRUST CO	4.70%	Yes	9846		22.0900
6		KENTUCKY BANK	4.43%	Yes	734		19.6249
7		TRADITIONAL BANK INC	4.27%	Yes	2711		18.2329
8	ST	WHITAKER BANK	3.54%	Yes	32912		12.5316
9		COMMUNITY TRUST BANK INC	2.53%	Yes	2720		6.4009
10		BANK OF BLUE GRASS & TR CO	2.53%	No	21161		6.4009
11		CITIZENS COMMERCE NB	2.47%	No	34256		6.1009
12		AMERICAN FOUNDERS BANK INC	2.40%	No	57113		5.7600
13		FARMERS B&T CO OF GEORGETOWN Ky	2.39%	No	10136		5.7121
14		REPUBLIC BANK & TRUST CO	2.29%	Yes	23627		5.2441
15		PNC BANK NATIONAL ASSN	2.05%	Comments	6384		4.2025
16		UNITED BANK & TRUST CO	2.05%	No	15608		4.2025
17		CITIZENS NB JESSAMINE CNTY	1.84%	No	34195		3.3856
18		CENTRAL BANK FSB	1.71%	No	34581		2.9241
19		U S BANK NATIONAL ASSN	1.34%	Yes	6548		1.7956
20		FIRST FEDERAL BANK	1.24%	No	29594		1.5376
21		FIRST NB OF LEXINGTON	1.06%	No	57415		1.1236
22		FARMERS BANK	1.01%	No	14894		1.0201
	A	Market Share of Banks Reviewed	**93.43%**	22	Banks reviewed HHI Points		776.9679
	B	MSA Mean Market Share Per Bank Reviewed	**4.25%**		RvB Actual HHI Points		540.2744
	C	MSA Median Market Share Per Bank Reviewed	**2.44%**				
	D	Market Share of Banks with Rent v. Buy calculator	58.74%	10	RvB Pro Forma HHI Points		**3450.3876**
	E	MSA Mean Market Share Per RvB Bank	5.87%				
	F	MSA Median Market Share for RvB Banks	4.35%		Leon L. Morris ©		

Legend	
Top 50 National Bank	
Market Share of Bank Reviewed	
Bank w. Rent v. Buy Calculator	
Calculator Performed Correctly	
Calculator Performed Incorrectly	
HHI Points	
Save in Taxes - Calculator	ST
No retail Mortgage loans solicited	NRML

Lexington

Herfendahl-Herschman	Index	# of Institutions
Actual	781.4255	35
Pro-Forma	3691.7228	26
Change > 100	**2910.2973**	

TABLE 18

	State	Louisiana
18	Metropolitan Area	New Orleans - Metairie – Kenner, LA

Rank		Institution Name	Market Share	Rent v. Buy (RvB) Calculator	FDIC Certificate #	Calculator Performance	Actual HHI Points
1	ST	CAPITAL ONE NATIONAL ASSN	29.08%	Yes	4297		845.6464
2		JP MORGAN CHASE BANK NA	19.12%	Yes	628		365.5744
3		WHITNEY NATIONAL BANK *	14.93%	Yes	18538		222.9049
4		REGIONS BANK	7.76%	Yes	12368		60.2176
5		AMSOUTH BANK	3.18%	Yes	26800		10.1124
6		FIDELITY HOMESTEAD ASSN	2.58%	**No**	28316		6.6564
7	ST	GULF COAST BANK & TRUST	2.19%	Yes	32974		4.7961
8		OMNI BANK	1.87%	**No**	27397		3.4969
9		FIRST BANK & TRUST	1.87%	NRML	33405		3.4969
10		PARISH NATIONAL BANK	1.75%	**No**	19783		3.0625
11		IBERIABANK	1.44%	Yes	28100		2.0736
12		HANCOCK BANK OF LOUISIANA	1.39%	Yes	33029		1.9321
13		FIFTH DISTRICT SAVINGS BANK	1.16%	**No**	27697		1.3456
14		METAIRE BANK & TRUST	1.13%	**No**	16539		1.2769
15		FIRST AMERICAN BANK & TRUST	1.12%	**No**	8149		1.2544
16		CRESCENT BANK AND TRUST	1.06%	NRML	33492		1.1236
17		CENTRAL PROGESSIVE BANK	1.01%	**No**	19657		1.0201
	A	Market Share of Banks Reviewed	**92.64%**	17	Banks reviewed HHI Points		1535.9908
	B	MSA Mean Market Share Per Bank Reviewed	**5.45%**		RvB Actual HHI Points		1513.2575
	C	MSA Median Market Share Per Bank Reviewed	**1.87%**				
	D	Market Share of Banks with Rent v. Buy calculator	79.09%	8	RvB Pro Forma HHI Points		**6255.2281**
	E	MSA Mean Market Share Per RvB Bank	9.89%				
	F	MSA Median Market Share for RvB Banks	5.47%		Leon L. Morris ©		

Legend	
Top 50 National Bank	
Market Share of Bank Reviewed	
Bank w. Rent v. Buy Calculator	
Calculator Performed Correctly	
Calculator Performed Incorrectly	
HHI Points	
Save in Taxes - Calculator	ST
No retail Mortgage loans solicited	NRML

*link to Freddie Mac Calculator

Entire New Orleans MSA

Herfendahl-Herschman	Index	# of Institutions
Actual	1539.3939	42
Pro-Forma	6281.0394	35
Change > 100	**4741.6455**	

TABLE 19

19	State	Maine
	Metropolitan Area	Portland - South Portland - Biddeford, ME

Rank		Institution Name	Market Share	Rent v. Buy (RvB) Calculator	FDIC Certificate #	Calculator Performance	Actual HHI Points
1		TD BANKNORTH NATIONAL ASSN	26.59%	Yes	18409		707.0281
2		KEYBANK NATIONAL ASSN	16.21%	Yes	17534		262.7641
3		BANK OF AMERICA NA	12.74%	Yes	3510		162.3076
4		KENNEBUNK SAVINGS BANK	6.80%	Yes	13063		46.2400
5		GORHAM SAVINGS BANK	5.65%	Yes	17748		31.9225
6		SACO&BIDDEFORD SVG INST	5.03%	**No**	17743		25.3009
7		NORWAY SAVINGS BANK	4.74%	**No**	17658		22.4676
8		MAINE BANK & TRUST CO	3.38%	**No**	33525		11.4244
9		BATH SAVINGS INSTITUTION	3.31%	Yes	17749		10.9561
10		SANFORD INST FOR SVG	3.01%	**No**	17115		9.0601
11		OCEAN NATIONAL BANK	2.57%	**No**	4264		6.6049
12		BIDDEFORD SAVINGS BANK	2.26%	**No**	17741		5.1076
13		GARDINER SVG INST FSB	1.49%	**No**	19686		2.2201
14		CAMDEN NATIONAL BANK	1.25%	Yes	4255		1.5625
15		NORTHEAST BANK	1.20%	**No**	19690		1.4400
	A	Market Share of Banks Reviewed	**96.23%**	15	Banks reviewed HHI Points		1306.4065
	B	MSA Mean Market Share Per Bank Reviewed	**6.42%**		RvB Actual HHI Points		1222.7809
	C	MSA Median Market Share Per Bank Reviewed	**3.38%**				
	D	Market Share of Banks with Rent v. Buy calculator	72.55%	7	RvB Pro Forma HHI Points		**5263.5025**
	E	MSA Mean Market Share Per RvB Bank	10.36%				
	F	MSA Median Market Share for RvB Banks	6.80%		Leon L. Morris ©		

Legend	
Top 50 National Bank	
Market Share of Bank Reviewed	
Bank w. Rent v. Buy Calculator	
Calculator Performed Correctly	
Calculator Performed Incorrectly	
HHI Points	
Save in Taxes - Calculator	ST
No retail Mortgage loans solicited	NRML

Portland, Maine		
Herfendahl-Herschman	**Index**	# of Institutions
Actual	1309.0473	23
Pro-Forma	5350.4532	17
Change > 100	**4041.4059**	

TABLE 20

20	State	Maryland
	Metropolitan Area	Baltimore-Townsend, MD

Rank		Institution Name	Market Share	Rent v. Buy (RvB) Calculator	FDIC Certificate #	Calculator Performance	Actual HHI Points
1		BANK OF AMERICA NA	23.78%	Yes	3510		565.4884
2		MANUFACTURERS & TRADERS TR CO	10.79%	No	588		116.4241
3		MERCANTILE-SAFE DEPOSIT & TR	8.68%	No	20347		75.3424
4		WACHOVIA BANK NATIONAL ASSN	8.19%	No	33869		67.0761
5		PROVIDENT BANK OF MARYLAND	5.84%	Yes	15951		34.1056
6		BRANCH BANKING & TRUST CO	5.49%	Yes	9846		30.1401
7		SUNTRUST BANK	3.61%	Yes	867		13.0321
8		SUSQUEHANNA BANK	2.05%	No	9694		4.2025
9	ST	FIRST MARINER BANK	1.90%	Yes	31286		3.6100
10		EASTERN SAVINGS BANK FSB	1.65%	No	32360		2.7225
11		COLUMBIA BANK	1.58%	No	27244		2.4964
12		WESTMINSTER UNION BANK	1.50%	No	12884		2.2500
13		SEVERN SAVINGS BANK FSB	1.38%	No	32367		1.9044
14		BALTIMORE COUNTY SB FSB	1.36%	No	32341		1.8496
15		K BANK	1.21%	No	31263		1.4641
16		CITIZENS NATIONAL BANK	1.21%	No	4852		1.4641
17	ST	CHEVY CHASE BANK FSB	1.11%	Yes	32324		1.2321
	A	Market Share of Banks Reviewed	**81.33%**	17	Banks reviewed HHI Points		924.8045
	B	MSA Mean Market Share Per Bank Reviewed	**4.78%**		RvB Actual HHI Points		647.6083
	C	MSA Median Market Share Per Bank Reviewed	**1.90%**				
	D	Market Share of Banks with Rent v. Buy calculator	41.73%	6	RvB Pro Forma HHI Points		**1741.3929**
	E	MSA Mean Market Share Per RvB Bank	6.96%				
	F	MSA Median Market Share for RvB Banks	4.55%		Leon L. Morris ©		

Legend	
Top 50 National Bank	
Market Share of Bank Reviewed	
Bank w. Rent v. Buy Calculator	
Calculator Performed Correctly	
Calculator Performed Incorrectly	
HHI Points	
Save in Taxes - Calculator	ST
No retail Mortgage loans solicited	NRML

Entire Baltimore MSA		
Herfendahl-Herschman	**Index**	# of Institutions
Actual	934.2498	90
Pro-Forma	2027.8939	85
Change > 100	**1093.6441**	

TABLE 21

21	State	Massachusetts
	Metropolitan Area	Boston-Cambridge-Quincy, MA

Rank		Institution Name	Market Share	Rent v. Buy (RvB) Calculator	FDIC Certificate #	Calculator Performance	Actual HHI Points
1		BANK OF AMERICA NA	20.63%	Yes	3510		425.5969
2	ST	CITIZENS BANK OF MA	16.59%	Yes	18562		275.2281
3		STATE STREET BANK & TRUST CO	8.42%	NRML	14		70.8964
4	5	SOVEREIGN BANK	6.61%	Yes	29950		43.6921
5		MELLON TR OF NEW ENGLAND NA	5.82%	NRML	22295		33.8724
6		INVESTORS BANK & TRUST CO	4.15%	NRML	20072		17.2225
7		TD BANKNORTH NATIONAL ASSN	3.79%	Yes	18409		14.3641
8		EASTERN BANK	3.22%	Yes	32773		10.3684
9		MIDDLESEX SAVINGS BANK	2.09%	Yes	90183		4.3681
10		CAMBRIDGE SAVINGS BANK	1.18%	Yes	17870		1.3924
11		CITIZENSBANK NEW HAMPSHIRE	1.16%	Yes	6214		1.3456
12		SALEM FIVE CENTS SB	1.13%	Yes	23296		1.2769
13		ROCKLAND TRUST CO	1.08%	**No**	9712		1.1664
14		BOSTON PRIVATE BANK & TRUST CO	1.07%	**No**	24811		1.1449
	A	Market Share of Banks Reviewed	**76.94%**	14	Banks reviewed HHI Points		901.9352
	B	MSA Mean Market Share Per Bank Reviewed	**5.50%**		RvB Actual HHI Points		777.6326
	C	MSA Median Market Share Per Bank Reviewed	**3.51%**				
	D	Market Share of Banks with Rent v. Buy calculator	56.40%	9	RvB Pro Forma HHI Points		**3180.9600**
	E	MSA Mean Market Share Per RvB Bank	6.27%				
	F	MSA Median Market Share for RvB Banks	3.22%		Leon L. Morris ©		

Legend	
Top 50 National Bank	
Market Share of Bank Reviewed	
Bank w. Rent v. Buy Calculator	
Calculator Performed Correctly	
Calculator Performed Incorrectly	
HHI Points	
Save in Taxes - Calculator	ST
No retail Mortgage loans solicited	NRML

Entire Boston MSA

Herfendahl-Herschman	Index	# of Institutions
Actual	909.7003	157
Pro-Forma	3313.0241	149
Change > 100	**2403.3238**	

TABLE 22

22	State	Michigan
	Metropolitan Area	Detroit- Warren-Livonia, MI

Rank		Institution Name	Market Share	Rent v. Buy (RvB) Calculator	FDIC Certificate #	Calculator Performance	Actual HHI Points
1	ST	LASALLE BANK MIDWEST NA	23.00%	Yes	22488		529.0000
2		COMERICA BANK	22.80%	No	983		519.8400
3		JP MORGAN CHASE BANK NA	14.76%	Yes	628		217.8576
4		FLAGSTAR BANK FSB	6.53%	Yes	32541		42.6409
5		NATIONAL CITY BANK OF THE MW	6.49%	Yes	5029		42.1201
6	ST	CHARTER ONE BANK NA	6.22%	Yes	28932		38.6884
7	ST	FIFTH THIRD BANK	4.78%	Yes	993		22.8484
8		HUNTINGTON NATIONAL BANK	2.69%	Yes	6560		7.2361
9	ST	CITIZENS FIRST SAVINGS BANK	1.12%	**No**	30005		1.2544
	A	Market Share of Banks Reviewed	**88.39%**	9	Banks reviewed HHI Points		1421.4859
	B	MSA Mean Market Share Per Bank Reviewed	**9.82%**		RvB Actual HHI Points		900.3915
	C	MSA Median Market Share Per Bank Reviewed	**6.49%**				
	D	Market Share of Banks with Rent v. Buy calculator	64.47%	7	RvB Pro Forma HHI Points		**4156.3809**
	E	MSA Mean Market Share Per RvB Bank	9.21%				
	F	MSA Median Market Share for RvB Banks	6.49%		Leon L. Morris ©		

Legend	
Top 50 National Bank	
Market Share of Bank Reviewed	
Bank w. Rent v. Buy Calculator	
Calculator Performed Correctly	
Calculator Performed Incorrectly	
HHI Points	
Save in Taxes - Calculator	ST
No retail Mortgage loans solicited	NRML

Entire Detroit MSA		
Herfendahl-Herschman	**Index**	# of Institutions
Actual	1426.9336	61
Pro-Forma	4684.3077	55
Change > 100	**3257.3741**	

TABLE 23

23	State	Minnesota				
	Metropolitan Area	Minneapolis - St. Paul-Bloomington, MN-WI				

Rank		Institution Name	Market Share	Rent v. Buy (RvB) Calculator	FDIC Certificate #	Calculator Performance	Actual HHI Points
1		WELLS FARGO BANK NA	27.98%	Yes	3511		782.8804
2		U S BANK NATIONAL ASSN	26.64%	Yes	6548		709.6896
3		TCF NATIONAL BANK	6.32%	No	28330		39.9424
4		M&I MARSHALL&ILSLEY BANK	2.97%	Yes	1020		8.8209
5	ST	BREMER BANK NATIONAL ASN	2.78%	**No**	12923		7.7284
6	ST	ASSOCIATED BANK NA	1.99%	Yes	5296		3.9601
7		KLEINBANK	1.51%	Yes	1414		2.2801
	A	Market Share of Banks Reviewed	**70.19%**	7	Banks reviewed HHI Points		1555.3019
	B	MSA Mean Market Share Per Bank Reviewed	**10.03%**		RvB Actual HHI Points		1507.6311
	C	MSA Median Market Share Per Bank Reviewed	**2.97%**				
	D	Market Share of Banks with Rent v. Buy calculator	61.09%	5	RvB Pro Forma HHI Points		**3731.9881**
	E	MSA Mean Market Share Per RvB Bank	12.22%				
	F	MSA Median Market Share for RvB Banks	2.97%		Leon L. Morris ©		

Legend	
Top 50 National Bank	
Market Share of Bank Reviewed	
Bank w. Rent v. Buy Calculator	
Calculator Performed Correctly	
Calculator Performed Incorrectly	
HHI Points	
Save in Taxes - Calculator	ST
No retail Mortgage loans solicited	NRML

Entire Minneapolis MSA

Herfendahl-Herschman	Index	# of Institutions
Actual	1565.8816	183
Pro-Forma	4130.3483	178
Change > 100	**2564.4667**	

TABLE 24

24	State	Mississippi
	Metropolitan Area	Jackson, MS

Rank		Institution Name	Market Share	Rent v. Buy (RvB) Calculator	FDIC Certificate #	Calculator Performance	Actual HHI Points
1		TRUSTMARK NATIONAL BANK	37.21%	Yes	4988		1384.5841
2		AMSOUTH BANK	19.28%	Yes	26800		371.7184
3		BANCORPSOUTH BANK	8.50%	No	11813		72.2500
4		BANKPLUS	7.62%	Yes	5903		58.0644
5		REGIONS BANK	6.02%	Yes	12368		36.2404
6		COMMUNITY BANK OF MS	3.96%	No	8879		15.6816
7	ST	MERCHANT & FARMERS BANK	3.89%	Yes	9361		15.1321
8		PRIORITYONE BANK	2.21%	No	21906		4.8841
9		FIRST COMMERCIAL BANK	1.77%	No	57069		3.1329
10		STATE BANK & TRUST CO	1.57%	No	8878		2.4649
11		PEOPLES BANK	1.28%	No	9366		1.6384
12		WACHOVIA BANK NATIONAL ASSN	1.19%	No	33869		1.4161
13		COPIAH BANK NATIONAL ASSN	1.15%	No	8231		1.3225
	A	Market Share of Banks Reviewed	**95.65%**	13	Banks reviewed HHI Points		1968.5299
	B	MSA Mean Market Share Per Bank Reviewed	**7.36%**		RvB Actual HHI Points		1865.7394
	C	MSA Median Market Share Per Bank Reviewed	**3.89%**				
	D	Market Share of Banks with Rent v. Buy calculator	74.02%	5	RvB Pro Forma HHI Points		**5478.9604**
	E	MSA Mean Market Share Per RvB Bank	14.80%				
	F	MSA Median Market Share for RvB Banks	7.62%		Leon L. Morris ©		

Legend	
Top 50 National Bank	
Market Share of Bank Reviewed	
Bank w. Rent v. Buy Calculator	
Calculator Performed Correctly	
Calculator Performed Incorrectly	
HHI Points	
Save in Taxes - Calculator	ST
No retail Mortgage loans solicited	NRML

Jackson

Herfendahl-Herschman	Index	# of Institutions
Actual	1971.004	23
Pro-Forma	5584.1833	19
Change > 100	**3613.1793**	

TABLE 25

25	State	Missouri
	Metropolitan Area	Kansas City, MO-KS

Rank		Institution Name	Market Share	Rent v. Buy (RvB) Calculator	FDIC Certificate #	Calculator Performance	Actual HHI Points
1		BANK OF AMERICA NA	9.93%	Yes	3510		98.6049
2		COMMERCE BANK NATIONAL ASSN	9.31%	Yes	24998		86.6761
3		UMB BANK NATIONAL ASSN	9.17%	Yes	8273		84.0889
4		U S BANK NATIONAL ASSN	5.14%	Yes	6548		26.4196
5		M&I MARSHALL&ISLEY BANK	4.63%	Yes	1020		21.4369
6		CAPITOL FEDERAL SAVINGS BANK	4.43%	No	27981		19.6249
7		BANK MIDWEST NATIONAL ASSN	3.79%	Yes	32964		14.3641
8	ST	HILLCREST BANK	3.17%	Yes	22173		10.0489
9	ST	FIRST NB OF KANSAS	2.70%	Yes	33789		7.2900
10		WORLD SAVINGS BANK FSB	2.31%	No	27076		5.3361
11		FIRST NATIONAL BANK OF OLA	2.28%	No	4744		5.1984
12		BANK OF BLUE VALLEY	1.58%	No	32722		2.4964
13		UNION BANK	1.54%	No	19582		2.3716
14	ST	VALLEY VIEW STATE BANK	1.46%	Yes	19631		2.1316
15	ST	BANK OF THE WEST	1.43%	Yes	3514		2.0449
16		BLUE RIDGE BANK & TRUST CO	1.22%	No	17933		1.4884
17		COUNTRY CLUB BANK NA	1.20%	Yes	17398		1.4400
18		SECURITY BANK OF KANSAS CITY	1.13%	No	4705		1.2769
19		BROTHERHOOD BANK & TRUST CO	1.12%	No	1874		1.2544
20		NATIONAL BANK OF KANSAS CITY	1.09%	No	35014		1.1881
	A	Market Share of Banks Reviewed	**68.63%**	20	Banks reviewed HHI Points		394.7811
	B	MSA Mean Market Share Per Bank Reviewed	**3.43%**		RvB Actual HHI Points		354.5459
	C	MSA Median Market Share Per Bank Reviewed	**2.30%**				
	D	Market Share of Banks with Rent v. Buy calculator	51.93%	11	RvB Pro Forma HHI Points		**2696.7249**
	E	MSA Mean Market Share Per RvB Bank	4.72%				
	F	MSA Median Market Share for RvB Banks	3.79%		Leon L. Morris ©		

Legend	
Top 50 National Bank	
Market Share of Bank Reviewed	
Bank w. Rent v. Buy Calculator	
Calculator Performed Correctly	
Calculator Performed Incorrectly	
HHI Points	
Save in Taxes - Calculator	ST
No retail Mortgage loans solicited	NRML

Entire Kansas City MSA

Herfendahl-Herschman	Index	# of Institutions
Actual	408.1862	150
Pro-Forma	2718.9531	146
Change > 100	**2310.4679**	

TABLE 26

26	State	Montana
	Metropolitan Area	Billings, MT

Rank		Institution Name	Market Share	Rent v. Buy (RvB) Calculator	FDIC Certificate #	Calculator Performance	Actual HHI Points
1		FIRST INTERSTATE BANK	31.87%	Yes	1105		1015.6969
2		WELLS FARGO BANK NA	12.55%	Yes	3511		157.5025
3		WESTERN SECURITY BANK	10.61%	No	57248		112.5721
4		STOCKMAN BANK OF MONTANA	9.61%	Yes	16191		92.3521
5		U S BANK NATIONAL ASSN	9.35%	Yes	6548		87.4225
6		YELLOWSTONE BANK	8.94%	No	1978		79.9236
7		FIRST CITIZENS BK BILLINGS merging w/ Western Security -2007	6.46%	No	19964		41.7316
8		ROCKY MOUNTAIN BANK	3.82%	No	20310		14.5924
9		STERLING SAVINGS BANK	2.29%	No	32158		5.2441
10		BANK OF BRIDGER NA	1.92%	No	2224		3.6864
11		HERITAGEBANK	1.27%	No	34970		1.6129
12		LITTLE HORN STATE BANK	1.12%	No	11821		1.2544
	A	Market Share of Banks Reviewed	**99.81%**	12	Banks reviewed HHI Points		1613.5915
	B	MSA Mean Market Share Per Bank Reviewed	**8.32%**		RvB Actual HHI Points		1352.9740
	C	MSA Median Market Share Per Bank Reviewed	**7.70%**				
	D	Market Share of Banks with Rent v. Buy calculator	63.38%	4	RvB Pro Forma HHI Points		**4017.0244**
	E	MSA Mean Market Share Per RvB Bank	15.85%				
	F	MSA Median Market Share for RvB Banks	11.08%		Leon L. Morris ©		

Legend	
Top 50 National Bank	
Market Share of Bank Reviewed	
Bank w. Rent v. Buy Calculator	
Calculator Performed Correctly	
Calculator Performed Incorrectly	
HHI Points	
Save in Taxes - Calculator	ST
No retail Mortgage loans solicited	NRML

Entire Billings MSA

Herfendahl-Herschman	Index	# of Institutions
Actual	1613.6276	13
Pro-Forma	4277.6780	10
Change > 100	**2664.0504**	

TABLE 27

27	State	Nebraska
	Metropolitan Area	Omaha-Council Bluffs, NE-IA

Rank		Institution Name	Market Share	Rent v. Buy (RvB) Calculator	FDIC Certificate #	Calculator Performance	Actual HHI Points
1		FIRST NATIONAL BANK OF OMAHA	31.31%	Yes	5452		980.3161
2		U S BANK NATIONAL ASSN	9.99%	Yes	6548		99.8001
3		WELLS FARGO BANK NA	9.79%	Yes	3511		95.8441
4		AMERICAN NATIONAL BANK	7.76%	Yes	19300		60.2176
5		GREAT WESTERN BANK	5.49%	Yes	8327		30.1401
6	ST	BANK OF THE WEST	5.29%	Yes	3514		27.9841
7		TIERONE BANK	3.26%	Yes	29341		10.6276
8		PINNACLE BANK	2.79%	No	10634		7.7841
9		SECURITY NB OF OMAHA	2.75%	No	19213		7.5625
10		NEBRASKA STATE BANK OF OMAHA	1.64%	No	20927		2.6896
11		OMAHA STATE BANK	1.36%	Yes	20628		1.8496
12		MID CITY BANK INC	1.25%	No	19397		1.5625
13		WASHINGTON COUNTY BANK	1.09%	No	12241		1.1881
14		MIDSTATE BANK NATIONAL ASSN	1.06%	Yes	4465		1.1236
	A	Market Share of Banks Reviewed	**84.83%**	14	Banks reviewed HHI Points		1328.6897
	B	MSA Mean Market Share Per Bank Reviewed	**6.06%**		RvB Actual HHI Points		1307.9029
	C	MSA Median Market Share Per Bank Reviewed	**3.03%**				
	D	Market Share of Banks with Rent v. Buy calculator	75.31%	9	RvB Pro Forma HHI Points		**5671.5961**
	E	MSA Mean Market Share Per RvB Bank	8.37%				
	F	MSA Median Market Share for RvB Banks	5.49%		Leon L. Morris ©		

Legend	
Top 50 National Bank	
Market Share of Bank Reviewed	
Bank w. Rent v. Buy Calculator	
Calculator Performed Correctly	
Calculator Performed Incorrectly	
HHI Points	
Save in Taxes - Calculator	ST
No retail Mortgage loans solicited	NRML

Entire Omaha MSA

Herfendahl-Herschman	Index	# of Institutions
Actual	1335.2406	74
Pro-Forma	5698.8956	66
Change > 100	**4363.6550**	

TABLE 28

28	State	Nevada
	Metropolitan Area	Las Vegas-Paradise, NV

Rank		Institution Name	Market Share	Rent v. Buy (RvB) Calculator	FDIC Certificate #	Calculator Performance	Actual HHI Points
1		WASHINGTON MUTUAL BANK	68.12%	Yes	32633		4640.3344
2		BANK OF AMERICA NA	6.89%	Yes	3510		47.4721
3		CITIBANK NEVADA NA	6.25%	Statement	26211		39.0625
4		WELLS FARGO BANK NA	5.18%	Yes	3511		26.8324
5	ST	NEVADA STATE BANK	2.23%	Yes	18113		4.9729
6		BANK OF NEVADA	2.10%	**No**	33897		4.4100
7		U S BANK NATIONAL ASSN	1.47%	Yes	6548		2.1609
	A	Market Share of Banks Reviewed	**92.24%**	**7**	Banks reviewed HHI Points		4765.2452
	B	MSA Mean Market Share Per Bank Reviewed	**13.18%**		RvB Actual HHI Points		4721.7727
	C	MSA Median Market Share Per Bank Reviewed	**5.18%**				
	D	Market Share of Banks with Rent v. Buy calculator	83.89%	**5**	RvB Pro Forma HHI Points		**7037.5321**
	E	MSA Mean Market Share Per RvB Bank	16.78%				
	F	MSA Median Market Share for RvB Banks	5.18%		Leon L. Morris ©		

Legend	
Top 50 National Bank	
Market Share of Bank Reviewed	
Bank w. Rent v. Buy Calculator	
Calculator Performed Correctly	
Calculator Performed Incorrectly	
HHI Points	
Save in Taxes - Calculator	ST
No retail Mortgage loans solicited	NRML

Las Vegas

Herfendahl-Herschman	**Index**	# of Institutions
Actual	4770.0908	41
Pro-Forma	7086.3036	37
Change > 100	**2316.2128**	

TABLE 29

Rank		Institution Name	Market Share	Rent v. Buy (RvB) Calculator	FDIC Certificate #	Calculator Performance	Actual HHI Points
29		State: New Hampshire					
		Metropolitan Area: Manchester-Nashua, NH					
1	ST	CITIZENS BANK NEW HAMPSHIRE	48.71%	Yes	6214		2372.6641
2		TD BANKNORTH NATIONAL ASSN	20.00%	Yes	18409		400.0000
3		BANK OF AMERICA NA	13.42%	Yes	3510		180.0964
4	4	SOVEREIGN BANK	5.85%	Yes	29950		34.2225
5		OCEAN NATIONAL BANK	4.47%	**No**	4264		19.9809
6		CENTRIX BANK & TRUST	3.38%	**No**	35035		11.4244
7		SOUTHERN NH B&T CO	2.13%	No	24540		4.5369
	A	Market Share of Banks Reviewed	**97.96%**	7	Banks reviewed HHI Points		3022.9252
	B	MSA Mean Market Share Per Bank Reviewed	**13.99%**		RvB Actual HHI Points		2986.9830
	C	MSA Median Market Share Per Bank Reviewed	**5.85%**				
	D	Market Share of Banks with Rent v. Buy calculator	87.98%	4	RvB Pro Forma HHI Points		**7740.4804**
	E	MSA Mean Market Share Per RvB Bank	22.00%				
	F	MSA Median Market Share for RvB Banks	16.71%		Leon L. Morris ©		

Legend	
Top 50 National Bank	
Market Share of Bank Reviewed	
Bank w. Rent v. Buy Calculator	
Calculator Performed Correctly	
Calculator Performed Incorrectly	
HHI Points	
Save in Taxes - Calculator	ST
No retail Mortgage loans solicited	NRML

Entire Manchester MSA

Herfendahl-Herschman	Index	# of Institutions
Actual	3023.7918	13
Pro-Forma	7777.2975	10
Change > 100	**4753.5057**	

TABLE 30

30	State	New Jersey
	Metropolitan Area	New York- New Jersey - Long Island, NY, NJ, PA

Rank		Institution Name	Market Share	Rent v. Buy (RvB) Calculator	FDIC Certificate #	Calculator Performance	Actual HHI Points
1		JP MORGAN CHASE BANK NA	26.37%	Yes	628		695.3769
2		CITIBANK NATIONAL ASSN	16.04%		7213		257.2816
3	ST	HSBC BANK USA NATIONAL ASSN	6.23%	Yes	57890		38.8129
4		BANK OF AMERICA NA	6.00%	Yes	3510		36.0000
5		BANK OF NEW YORK	4.47%	Yes	639		19.9809
6		NORTH FORK BANK Capital One sub	4.22%	Yes	15985		17.8084
7		WACHOVIA BANK NATIONAL ASSN	3.50%	**No**	33869		12.2500
8		WASHINGTON MUTUAL BANK	2.07%	Yes	32633		4.2849
9		COMMERCE BANK NATIONAL ASSN	2.02%	Yes	21140		4.0804
10		ASTORIA FS&LA	1.54%	Yes	29805		2.3716
11		PNC BANK NATIONAL ASSN	1.46%		6384		2.1316
12	ST	NEW YORK COMMUNITY BANK	1.36%	Yes	16022		1.8496
13		HUDSON CITY SAVINGS BANK	1.33%	**No**	13074		1.7689
14	ST	INDEPENDENCE COMMUNITY BANK	1.32%	Yes	16018		1.7424
15		DEUTSCHE BANK TR CO AMERICAS	1.29%	NRML	623		1.6641
16		TD BANK USA NATIONAL ASSN	1.07%	Yes	33947		1.1449
17	ST	VALLEY NATIONAL BANK	1.00%	Yes	9396		1.0000
	A	Market Share of Banks Reviewed	**81.29%**	17	Banks reviewed HHI Points		1099.5491
	B	MSA Mean Market Share Per Bank Reviewed	**4.78%**		RvB Actual HHI Points		824.4529
	C	MSA Median Market Share Per Bank Reviewed	**2.02%**				
	D	Market Share of Banks with Rent v. Buy calculator	57.67%	12	RvB Pro Forma HHI Points		**3325.8289**
	E	MSA Mean Market Share Per RvB Bank	4.81%				
	F	MSA Median Market Share for RvB Banks	2.05%		Leon L. Morris ©		

Legend	
Top 50 National Bank	
Market Share of Bank Reviewed	
Bank w. Rent v. Buy Calculator	
Calculator Performed Correctly	
Calculator Performed Incorrectly	
HHI Points	
Save in Taxes - Calculator	ST
No retail Mortgage loans solicited	NRML

Entire Newark – NY MSA

Herfendahl-Herschman	Index	# of Institutions
Actual	1105.8306	242
Pro-Forma	3606.2026	231
Change > 100	**2500.3720**	

North Fork owns Greenpoint mortgage funding. NF - has unique calculator -forces 28%Marginal Rate

TABLE 31

31	State	New Mexico
	Metropolitan Area	Albuquerque, NM

Rank		Institution Name	Market Share	Rent v. Buy (RvB) Calculator	FDIC Certificate #	Calculator Performance	Actual HHI Points
1		WELLS FARGO BANK NA	24.86%	Yes	3511		618.0196
2		BANK OF AMERICA NA	24.73%	Yes	3510		611.5729
3		FIRST COMMUNITY BANK	13.50%	**No**	12261		182.2500
4		BANK OF ALBUQUERQUE NA	11.69%	**No**	34992		136.6561
5	ST	BANK OF THE WEST	6.80%	Yes	3514		46.2400
6		CHARTER BANK	5.87%	Yes	32498		34.4569
7		COMPASS BANK	4.11%	Yes	19048		16.8921
8		NEW MEXICO BANK & TRUST	3.03%	**No**	34726		9.1809
9		BANK OF BELEN	1.19%	**No**	33616		1.4161
	A	Market Share of Banks Reviewed	**95.78%**	9	Banks reviewed HHI Points		1656.6846
	B	MSA Mean Market Share Per Bank Reviewed	**10.64%**		RvB Actual HHI Points		1327.1815
	C	MSA Median Market Share Per Bank Reviewed	**6.80%**				
	D	Market Share of Banks with Rent v. Buy calculator	66.37%	5	RvB Pro Forma HHI Points		4404.9769
	E	MSA Mean Market Share Per RvB Bank	13.27%				
	F	MSA Median Market Share for RvB Banks	6.80%		Leon L. Morris ©		

Legend	
Top 50 National Bank	(yellow)
Market Share of Bank Reviewed	(green)
Bank w. Rent v. Buy Calculator	(orange)
Calculator Performed Correctly	(light green)
Calculator Performed Incorrectly	(red)
HHI Points	(blue)
Save in Taxes – Calculator	ST
No retail Mortgage loans solicited	NRML

Entire Albuquerque MSA

Herfendahl-Herschman	Index	# of Institutions
Actual	1659.5141	22
Pro-Forma	4738.3304	18
Change > 100	**3078.8163**	

TABLE 32

32	State	New York
	Metropolitan Area	New York- New Jersey – Long Island, NY, NJ, PA

Rank		Institution Name	Market Share	Rent v. Buy (RvB) Calculator	FDIC Certificate #	Calculator Performance	Actual HHI Points
1		JP MORGAN CHASE BANK NA	26.37%	Yes	628		695.3769
2		CITIBANK NATIONAL ASSN	16.04%	Statement	7213		257.2816
3	ST	HSBC BANK USA NATIONAL ASSN	6.23%	Yes	57890		38.8129
4		BANK OF AMERICA NA	6.00%	Yes	3510		36.0000
5		BANK OF NEW YORK	4.47%	Yes	639		19.9809
6		NORTH FORK BANK Capital One sub	4.22%	Yes	15985		17.8084
7		WACHOVIA BANK NATIONAL ASSN	3.50%	**No**	33869		12.2500
8		WASHINGTON MUTUAL BANK	2.07%	Yes	32633		4.2849
9		COMMERCE BANK NATIONAL ASSN	2.02%	Yes	21140		4.0804
10		ASTORIA FS&LA	1.54%	Yes	29805		2.3716
11		PNC BANK NATIONAL ASSN	1.46%	comments	6384		2.1316
12	ST	NEW YORK COMMUNITY BANK	1.36%	Yes	16022		1.8496
13		HUDSON CITY SAVINGS BANK	1.33%	**No**	13074		1.7689
14	ST	INDEPENDENCE COMMUNITY BANK	1.32%	Yes	16018		1.7424
15		DEUTSCHE BANK TR CO AMERICAS	1.29%	NRML	623		1.6641
16		TD BANK USA NATIONAL ASSN	1.07%	Yes	33947		1.1449
17	ST	VALLEY NATIONAL BANK	1.00%	Yes	9396		1.0000
	A	Market Share of Banks Reviewed	**81.29%**	17	Banks reviewed HHI Points		1099.5491
	B	MSA Mean Market Share Per Bank Reviewed	**4.78%**		RvB Actual HHI Points		824.4529
	C	MSA Median Market Share Per Bank Reviewed	**2.02%**				
	D	Market Share of Banks with Rent v. Buy calculator	57.67%	12	RvB Pro Forma HHI Points		**3325.8289**
	E	MSA Mean Market Share Per RvB Bank	4.81%				
	F	MSA Median Market Share for RvB Banks	2.05%		Leon L. Morris ©		

Legend	
Top 50 National Bank	
Market Share of Bank Reviewed	
Bank w. Rent v. Buy Calculator	
Calculator Performed Correctly	
Calculator Performed Incorrectly	
HHI Points	
Save in Taxes - Calculator	ST
No retail Mortgage loans solicited	NRML

Entire New York - Newark MSA

Herfendahl-Herschman	Index	# of Institutions
Actual	1105.8306	242
Pro-Forma	3606.2026	231
Change > 100	**2500.3720**	

TABLE 33

33	State	North Carolina
	Metropolitan Area	Charlotte- Gastonia-Concord, NC-SC

Rank		Institution Name	Market Share	Rent v. Buy (RvB) Calculator	FDIC Certificate #	Calculator Performance	Actual HHI Points
1		WACHOVIA BANK NATIONAL ASN	63.81%	No	33869		4071.7161
2		BANK OF AMERICA NA	23.09%	1	3510		533.1481
3		BRANCH BANK & TRUST CO	3.09%	1	9846		9.5481
4		FIRST CHARTER BANK	2.37%	1	4886		5.6169
5		SUNTRUST BANK	1.32%	1	867		1.7424
6	ST	RBC CENTURA BANK	1.19%	1	33184		1.4161
	A	Market Share of Banks Reviewed	**94.87%**	6	Banks reviewed HHI Points		4623.1877
	B	MSA Mean Market Share Per Bank Reviewed	**15.81%**		RvB Actual HHI Points		551.4716
	C	MSA Median Market Share Per Bank Reviewed	**2.73%**				
	D	Market Share of Banks with Rent v. Buy calculator	31.06%	5	RvB Pro Forma HHI Points		**964.7236**
	E	MSA Mean Market Share Per RvB Bank	6.21%				
	F	MSA Median Market Share for RvB Banks	2.37%		Leon L. Morris ©		

Legend	
Top 50 National Bank	
Market Share of Bank Reviewed	
Bank w. Rent v. Buy Calculator	
Calculator Performed Correctly	
Calculator Performed Incorrectly	
HHI Points	
Save in Taxes - Calculator	ST
No retail Mortgage loans solicited	NRML

Entire Charlotte MSA

Herfendahl-Herschman	Index	# of Institutions
Actual	4625.7012	46
Pro-Forma	5038.8969	42
Change > 100	**413.1957**	

TABLE 34

34	State	North Dakota
	Metropolitan Area	Fargo, DK-NM

Rank		Institution Name	Market Share	Rent v. Buy (RvB) Calculator	FDIC Certificate #	Calculator Performance	Actual HHI Points
1		STATE BANK & TRUST	33.00%	Yes	19581		1089.0000
2		WELLS FARGO BANK NA	15.47%	Yes	3511		239.3209
3		U S BANK NATIONAL ASSN	9.78%	Yes	6548		95.6484
4		BREMER BANK NATIONAL ASSN	5.64%	No	34380		31.8096
5		ALERUS FINANCIAL NA	5.44%	No	3931		29.5936
6		GATE CITY BANK	5.42%	No	27774		29.3764
7		FIRST INTERNATIONAL B&T	4.78%	Yes	10248		22.8484
8	ST	BANK OF THE WEST	3.02%	Yes	3514		9.1204
9		NORTHWESTERN BANK NA	2.52%	No	9746		6.3504
10		FIRST STB OF NORTH DAKOTA	1.88%	Yes	8387		3.5344
11		VISIONBANK	1.86%	No	57892		3.4596
12		STATE BANK OF HAWLEY	1.65%	No	11409		2.7225
13		FIRST NATIONAL BANK	1.59%	No	5161		2.5281
14		WESTERN STATE BANK	1.34%	Yes	9123		1.7956
15		AMERICAN FEDERAL BANK	1.20%	No	29140		1.4400
	A	Market Share of Banks Reviewed	**94.59%**	15	Banks reviewed HHI Points		1568.5483
	B	MSA Mean Market Share Per Bank Reviewed	**6.31%**		RvB Actual HHI Points		1461.2681
	C	MSA Median Market Share Per Bank Reviewed	**3.02%**				
	D	Market Share of Banks with Rent v. Buy calculator	69.27%	7	RvB Pro Forma HHI Points		**4798.3329**
	E	MSA Mean Market Share Per RvB Bank	9.90%				
	F	MSA Median Market Share for RvB Banks	4.78%		Leon L. Morris ©		

Legend	
Top 50 National Bank	
Market Share of Bank Reviewed	
Bank w. Rent v. Buy Calculator	
Calculator Performed Correctly	
Calculator Performed Incorrectly	
HHI Points	
Save in Taxes - Calculator	ST
No retail Mortgage loans solicited	NRML

Entire Fargo MSA

Herfendahl-Herschman	Index	# of Institutions
Actual	1571.9141	25
Pro-Forma	4908.3524	19
Change > 100	**3336.4383**	

TABLE 35

35	State	Ohio
	Metropolitan Area	Columbus

Rank		Institution Name	Market Share	Rent v. Buy (RvB) Calculator	FDIC Certificate #	Calculator Performance	Actual HHI Points
1		HUNTINGTON NATIONAL BANK	27.51%	Yes	6560		756.8001
2		JP MORGAN CHASE BANK	20.92%	Yes	628		437.6464
3	ST	FIFTH THIRD BANK	12.69%	Yes	6672		161.0361
4		NATIONAL CITY BANK	8.68%	Yes	6557		75.3424
5		PARK NATIONAL BANK	4.19%	Yes	6653		17.5561
6		KEYBANK NATIONAL ASSN	3.70%	Yes	17534		13.6900
7		U S BANK NATIONAL ASSN	3.03%	Yes	6548		9.1809
8		OHIO SAVINGS BANK FSB	2.22%	Yes	29776		4.9284
9		DELAWARE COUNTY B&T CO	1.82%	site unavail.	16940		3.3124
10		HEARTLAND BANK	1.30%	No	9443		1.6900
11		COMMERCE NATIONAL BANK	1.19%	No	33433		1.4161
12		SKY BANK	1.07%	Yes	5982		1.1449
13		BANK ONE TRUST CO NA	1.05%	Yes	21377		1.1025
14		UNION SAVINGS BANK	1.00%	No	32296		1.0000
	A	Market Share of Banks Reviewed	90.37%	14	Banks reviewed HHI Points		1485.8463
	B	MSA Mean Market Share Per Bank Reviewed	6.46%		RvB Actual HHI Points		1478.4278
	C	MSA Median Market Share Per Bank Reviewed	2.63%				
	D	Market Share of Banks with Rent v. Buy calculator	85.06%	10	RvB Pro Forma HHI Points		7235.2036
	E	MSA Mean Market Share Per RvB Bank	8.51%				
	F	MSA Median Market Share for RvB Banks	3.95%		Leon L. Morris ©		

Legend	
Top 50 National Bank	
Market Share of Bank Reviewed	
Bank w. Rent v. Buy Calculator	
Calculator Performed Correctly	
Calculator Performed Incorrectly	
HHI Points	
Save in Taxes - Calculator	ST
No retail Mortgage loans solicited	NRML

Entire Columbus MSA

Herfendahl-Herschman	Index	# of Institutions
Actual	1490.3248	61
Pro-Forma	7248.9356	52
Change > 100	5758.6108	

TABLE 36

36	State	Oklahoma
	Metropolitan Area	Oklahoma City, OK

Rank		Institution Name	Market Share	Rent v. Buy (RvB) Calculator	FDIC Certificate #	Calculator Performance	Actual HHI Points
1	ST	MIDFIRST BANK	18.26%	Yes	4063		333.4276
2		BANK OF OKLAHOMA NA	9.24%	Yes	4214		85.3776
3		JP MORGAN CHASE BANK NA	9.03%	Yes	628		81.5409
4		BANK OF AMERICA NA	6.29%	Yes	3510		39.5641
5		BANCFIRST	5.96%	No	27476		35.0464
6		INTERNATIONAL BK OF COM	4.41%	No	19629		19.4481
7		ARVEST BANK	4.04%	No	8728		16.3216
8		COPPERMARK BANK	4.03%	No	18957		16.2409
9		FIRST FIDELITY BANK NA	3.19%	No	23473		10.1761
10		STILLWATER NB&T CO	2.42%	Yes	4201		5.8564
11		UNION BANK NATIONAL ASSN	1.92%	No	27210		3.6864
12		KIRKPATRICK BANK	1.67%	No	20156		2.7889
13		QUAIL CREEK BANK NA	1.61%	No	21848		2.5921
14		FRONTIER STATE BANK	1.58%	No	21978		2.4964
15	ST	FIRST NATIONAL BANK	1.56%	Yes	16127		2.4336
16		REPUBLIC BANK & TRUST	1.25%	No	27286		1.5625
17		FIRST NB&T CO CHICKASHA OK	1.25%	No	4062		1.5625
18		LEGACY BANK	1.24%	Yes	4042		1.5376
19		CITIZENS BANK OF EDMOND	1.15%	No	4084		1.3225
20		INTRUST BANK NATIONAL ASSN	1.14%	Yes	4799		1.2996
	A	Market Share of Banks Reviewed	**81.24%**	**20**	Banks reviewed HHI Points		664.2818
	B	MSA Mean Market Share Per Bank Reviewed	**4.06%**		RvB Actual HHI Points		551.0374
	C	MSA Median Market Share Per Bank Reviewed	**2.17%**				
	D	Market Share of Banks with Rent v. Buy calculator	49.18%	**8**	RvB Pro Forma HHI Points		**2418.6724**
	E	MSA Mean Market Share Per RvB Bank	6.15%				
	F	MSA Median Market Share for RvB Banks	4.36%		Leon L. Morris ©		

Legend	
Top 50 National Bank	
Market Share of Bank Reviewed	
Bank w. Rent v. Buy Calculator	
Calculator Performed Correctly	
Calculator Performed Incorrectly	
HHI Points	
Save in Taxes - Calculator	ST
No retail Mortgage loans solicited	NRML

Entire Oklahoma City MSA		
Herfendahl-Herschman	**Index**	# of Institutions
Actual	675.4735	67
Pro-Forma	2542.6582	60
Change > 100	**1867.1847**	

TABLE 37

37	State	Oregon
	Metropolitan Area	Portland-Vancouver-Beaverton, OR-WA

Rank		Institution Name	Market Share	Rent v. Buy (RvB) Calculator	FDIC Certificate #	Calculator Performance	Actual HHI Points
1		U S BANK NATIONAL ASSN	23.26%	Yes	6548		541.0276
2		BANK OF AMERICA NA	15.22%	Yes	3510		231.6484
3		WASHINGTON MUTUAL BANK	15.19%	Yes	32633		230.7361
4		WELLS FARGO BANK NA	14.81%	Yes	3511		219.3361
5		KEYBANK NATIONAL ASSN	8.56%	Yes	17534		73.2736
6		WEST COAST BANK	2.76%	No	2345		7.6176
7		FIRST INDEPENDENT BANK	2.38%	No	1500		5.6644
8		UMPQUA BANK	2.35%	Yes	17266		5.5225
9	ST	BANK OF THE WEST	1.91%	Yes	3514		3.6481
10		RIVERVIEW COMMUNITY BANK	1.86%	Yes	29922		3.4596
11		STERLING SAVINGS BANK	1.51%	No	32158		2.2801
12		WASHINGTON FS&LA	1.22%	No	28088		1.4884
	A	Market Share of Banks Reviewed	**91.03%**	12	Banks reviewed HHI Points		1325.7025
	B	MSA Mean Market Share Per Bank Reviewed	**7.59%**		RvB Actual HHI Points		1308.6520
	C	MSA Median Market Share Per Bank Reviewed	**2.57%**				
	D	Market Share of Banks with Rent v. Buy calculator	83.16%	8	RvB Pro Forma HHI Points		**6915.5856**
	E	MSA Mean Market Share Per RvB Bank	10.40%				
	F	MSA Median Market Share for RvB Banks	11.69%		Leon L. Morris ©		

Legend	
Top 50 National Bank	(yellow)
Market Share of Bank Reviewed	(green)
Bank w. Rent v. Buy Calculator	(orange)
Calculator Performed Correctly	(light green)
Calculator Performed Incorrectly	(red)
HHI Points	(blue)
Save in Taxes - Calculator	ST
No retail Mortgage loans solicited	NRML

Entire Portland Oregon MSA

Herfendahl-Herschman	Index	# of Institutions
Actual	1330.7678	42
Pro-Forma	6937.5638	35
Change > 100	**5606.7960**	

TABLE 38

38	State	Pennsylvania
	Metropolitan Area	Philadelphia-Camden-Wilmington, PA, NJ, DE, MD

Rank		Institution Name	Market Share	Rent v. Buy (RvB) Calculator	FDIC Certificate #	Calculator Performance	Actual HHI Points
1		ING BANK FSB	18.13%	No	6548		328.6969
2		CHASE BANK USA NATIONAL ASSN	10.58%	Yes	3510		111.9364
3		FIA CARD SERVICES NA Bank Of America	10.37%	Yes	32633		107.5369
4		WACHOVIA NATIONAL ASSN	8.68%	No	3511		75.3424
5		LEHMAN BROTHERS BANK FSB	6.40%	No	17534		40.9600
6		CITIZENS BANK OF PA	5.77%	Yes	2345		33.2929
7		COMMERCE BANK NATIONAL ASSN	5.45%	Yes	1500		29.7025
8	4	SOVEREIGN BANK	4.30%	Yes	17266		18.4900
9		PNC BANK NATIONAL ASSN	3.86%		3514		14.8996
10		BANK OF AMERICA NA	2.50%	Yes	29922		6.2500
11		GMAC BANK	2.50%	Yes	32158		6.2500
12	ST	WILMINGTON TRUST CO	2.43%	Yes	28088		5.9049
	A	Market Share of Banks Reviewed	**80.97%**	**12**	Banks reviewed HHI Points		779.2625
	B	MSA Mean Market Share Per Bank Reviewed	**6.75%**		RvB Actual HHI Points		319.3636
	C	MSA Median Market Share Per Bank Reviewed	**5.61%**				
	D	Market Share of Banks with Rent v. Buy calculator	43.90%	8	RvB Pro Forma HHI Points		**1927.2100**
	E	MSA Mean Market Share Per RvB Bank	5.49%				
	F	MSA Median Market Share for RvB Banks	4.88%		Leon L. Morris ©		

Legend	
Top 50 National Bank	
Market Share of Bank Reviewed	
Bank w. Rent v. Buy Calculator	
Calculator Performed Correctly	
Calculator Performed Incorrectly	
HHI Points	
Save in Taxes - Calculator	ST
No retail Mortgage loans solicited	NRML

Entire Philadelphia MSA

Herfendahl-Herschman	Index	# of Institutions
Actual	786.3196	158
Pro-Forma	2392.6522	151
Change > 100	**1606.3326**	

TABLE 39

39	State	Rhode Island
	Metropolitan Area	Providence-New Bedford - Fall River, RI - MA

Rank		Institution Name	Market Share	Rent v. Buy (RvB) Calculator	FDIC Certificate #	Calculator Performance	Actual HHI Points
1	ST	CITIZENS BANK OF RI	33.30%	Yes	16954		1108.8900
2		BANK OF AMERICA NA	15.92%	Yes	3510		253.4464
3	ST	SOVEREIGN BANK	10.58%	Yes	29950		111.9364
4		METLIFE BANK NATIONAL ASSN	7.43%	Yes	35055		55.2049
5		WASHINGTON TR CO OF WESTERLY	5.15%	Yes	23623		26.5225
6		WEBSTER BANK NATIONAL ASSN	4.37%	Yes	18221		19.0969
7		BANK RHODE ISLAND	3.19%	No	34147		10.1761
8	ST	CITIZENS BANK OF MA	2.34%	Yes	18562		5.4756
9		BANKNEWPORT	2.28%	No	18129		5.1984
10		BRISTOL COUNTY SAVINGS BANK	2.14%	No	23622		4.5796
11		CENTERVILLE SAVINGS BANK	1.84%	No	17764		3.3856
12		BANKFIVE	1.44%	Yes	23286		2.0736
13		CITIZENS-UNION SAVINGS BANK	1.42%	Yes	90196		2.0164
14		SLADES FERRY TRUST CO	1.39%	No	18085		1.9321
15		NORTH EASTON SAVINGS BANK	1.18%	No	90259		1.3924
	A	Market Share of Banks Reviewed	**93.97%**	15	Banks reviewed HHI Points		1611.3269
	B	MSA Mean Market Share Per Bank Reviewed	**6.26%**		RvB Actual HHI Points		1584.6627
	C	MSA Median Market Share Per Bank Reviewed	**2.34%**				
	D	Market Share of Banks with Rent v. Buy calculator	81.95%	9	RvB Pro Forma HHI Points		**6715.8025**
	E	MSA Mean Market Share Per RvB Bank	9.11%				
	F	MSA Median Market Share for RvB Banks	5.15%		Leon L. Morris ©		

Legend	
Top 50 National Bank	
Market Share of Bank Reviewed	
Bank w. Rent v. Buy Calculator	
Calculator Performed Correctly	
Calculator Performed Incorrectly	
HHI Points	
Save in Taxes - Calculator	ST
No retail Mortgage loans solicited	NRML

Entire Providence MSA

Herfendahl-Herschman	Index	# of Institutions
Actual	1613.9869	40
Pro-Forma	6745.124	32
Change > 100	**5131.1371**	

TABLE 40

40	State	South Carolina
	Metropolitan Area	Columbia, SC

Rank		Institution Name	Market Share	Rent v. Buy (RvB) Calculator	FDIC Certificate #	Calculator Performance	Actual HHI Points
1		WACHOVIA BANK NATIONAL ASSN	23.68%	**No**	33869		560.7424
2		BANK OF AMERICA NA	20.80%	Yes	3510		432.6400
3		BRANCH B&T CO OF SC	13.73%	Yes	21098		188.5129
4		NATIONAL BANK OF SC	12.19%	**No**	2111		148.5961
5		FIRST CITIZENS B&T CO INC	8.18%	Yes	15504		66.9124
6		CAROLINA FIRST BANK	6.82%	Yes	26849		46.5124
7		FIRST PALMETTO SB FSB	3.71%	**No**	28396		13.7641
8		FIRST COMMUNITY BANK NA	2.47%	**No**	34047		6.1009
9		CAROLINA NB&T CO	1.41%	No	57355		1.9881
10		SOUTH CAROLINA B&T NA	1.37%	No	13425		1.8769
	A	Market Share of Banks Reviewed	94.36%	10	Banks reviewed HHI Points		1467.6462
	B	MSA Mean Market Share Per Bank Reviewed	9.44%		RvB Actual HHI Points		734.5777
	C	MSA Median Market Share Per Bank Reviewed	7.50%				
	D	Market Share of Banks with Rent v. Buy calculator	49.53%	4	RvB Pro Forma HHI Points		**2453.2209**
	E	MSA Mean Market Share Per RvB Bank	12.38%				
	F	MSA Median Market Share for RvB Banks	10.96%		Leon L. Morris ©		

Legend	
Top 50 National Bank	
Market Share of Bank Reviewed	
Bank w. Rent v. Buy Calculator	
Calculator Performed Correctly	
Calculator Performed Incorrectly	
HHI Points	
Save in Taxes – Calculator	ST
No retail Mortgage loans solicited	NRML

Entire Columbia MSA

Herfendahl-Herschman	Index	# of Institutions
Actual	1470.5946	24
Pro-Forma	3189.926	21
Change > 100	**1719.3314**	

TABLE 41

41	State	South Dakota
	Metropolitan Area	Sioux Falls, SD

Rank		Institution Name	Market Share	Rent v. Buy (RvB) Calculator	FDIC Certificate #	Calculator Performance	Actual HHI Points
1		WELLS FARGO BANK NA	90.19%	Yes	3511		8134.2361
2		CITIBANK USA NATIONAL ASSN	2.51%	No	16100		6.3001
3		CITIBANK SOUTH DAKOTA NA	1.39%	No	23360		1.9321
	A	Market Share of Banks Reviewed	**94.09%**	3	Banks reviewed HHI Points		8142.4683
	B	MSA Mean Market Share Per Bank Reviewed	**31.36%**		RvB Actual HHI Points		8134.2361
	C	MSA Median Market Share Per Bank Reviewed	**2.51%**				
	D	Market Share of Banks with Rent v. Buy calculator	90.19%	1	RvB Pro Forma HHI Points		8134.2361
	E	MSA Mean Market Share Per RvB Bank	90.19%				
	F	MSA Median Market Share for RvB Banks	90.19%		Leon L. Morris ©		

Legend	
Top 50 National Bank	
Market Share of Bank Reviewed	
Bank w. Rent v. Buy Calculator	
Calculator Performed Correctly	
Calculator Performed Incorrectly	
HHI Points	
Save in Taxes - Calculator	ST
No retail Mortgage loans solicited	NRML

Entire Sioux Falls MSA

Herfendahl-Herschman	Index	# of Institutions
Actual	8145.2937	33
Pro-Forma	8145.2937	33
Change > 100	**0.0000**	

TABLE 42

42	State	Tennessee
	Metropolitan Area	Memphis, TN- MS- AR

Rank		Institution Name	Market Share	Rent v. Buy (RvB) Calculator	FDIC Certificate #	Calculator Performance	Actual HHI Points
1	ST	FIRST TENNESSEE BANK NA	52.54%	Yes	4977		2760.4516
2		REGIONS BANK	10.52%	Yes	12368		110.6704
3		SUNTRUST BANK	6.60%	Yes	867		43.5600
4		BANCORPSOUTH BANK	3.60%	**No**	11813		12.9600
5		BANK OF AMERICA NA	2.53%	Yes	3510		6.4009
6		AMSOUTH BANK	2.48%	Yes	26800		6.1504
7	ST	TRUSTMARK NATIONAL BANK	1.90%	Yes	4988		3.6100
8		INDEPENDENT BANK	1.66%	Yes	34728		2.7556
9		RENASANT BANK	1.54%	Yes	12437		2.3716
10	ST	BANK OF BARTLETT	1.46%	Yes	23123		2.1316
11		TRUST ONE BANK	1.42%	**No**	34059		2.0164
	A	Market Share of Banks Reviewed	**86.25%**	11	Banks reviewed HHI Points		2953.0785
	B	MSA Mean Market Share Per Bank Reviewed	**7.84%**		RvB Actual HHI Points		2938.1021
	C	MSA Median Market Share Per Bank Reviewed	**2.48%**				
	D	Market Share of Banks with Rent v. Buy calculator	81.23%	9	RvB Pro Forma HHI Points		**6598.3129**
	E	MSA Mean Market Share Per RvB Bank	9.03%				
	F	MSA Median Market Share for RvB Banks	2.48%		Leon L. Morris ©		

Legend	
Top 50 National Bank	
Market Share of Bank Reviewed	
Bank w. Rent v. Buy Calculator	
Calculator Performed Correctly	
Calculator Performed Incorrectly	
HHI Points	
Save in Taxes - Calculator	ST
No retail Mortgage loans solicited	NRML

Entire Memphis MSA

Herfendahl-Herschman	Index	# of Institutions
Actual	2959.9872	56
Pro-Forma	6620.1980	48
Change > 100	**3660.2108**	

TABLE 43

43	State	Texas
	Metropolitan Area	Houston-Baytown-Sugarland, TX

Rank		Institution Name	Market Share	Rent v. Buy (RvB) Calculator	FDIC Certificate #	Calculator Performance	Actual HHI Points
1		JP MORGAN CHASE BANK NA	29.31%	Yes	628		859.0761
2		BANK OF AMERICA NA	10.29%	Yes	3510		105.8841
3		WELLS FARGO BANK NA	8.83%	Yes	3511		77.9689
4		AMEGY BANK NATIONAL ASSN	5.79%	Yes	24107		33.5241
5		WASHINGTON MUTUAL BANK	5.20%	Yes	32633		27.0400
6		COMPASS BANK	3.59%	Yes	19048		12.8881
7		STERLING BANK	2.87%	Yes	21726		8.2369
8		PROSPERITY BANK	2.08%	Yes	16835		4.3264
9		WORLD SAVINGS BANK FSB	2.03%	**No**	27076		4.1209
10		FROST NATIONAL BANK	1.98%	**No**	5510		3.9204
11		WOODFOREST NATIONAL BANK	1.82%	Yes	23220		3.3124
12		GUARANTY BANK	1.78%	No	32618		3.1684
13		WORLD SAVINGS BANK FSB TEXAS	1.39%	No	33966		1.9321
14		FRANKLIN BANK SSB	1.33%	**No**	26870		1.7689
15	ST	CAPITAL ONE NATIONAL ASSN	1.25%	Yes	4297		1.5625
16		BANK OF TEXAS NATIONAL ASSN	1.18%	No	21674		1.3924
17		WACHOVIA BANK NATIONAL ASSN	1.11%	No	33869		1.2321
	A	Market Share of Banks Reviewed	81.83%	17	Banks reviewed HHI Points		1151.3547
	B	MSA Mean Market Share Per Bank Reviewed	4.81%		RvB Actual HHI Points		1133.8195
	C	MSA Median Market Share Per Bank Reviewed	2.03%				
	D	Market Share of Banks with Rent v. Buy calculator	71.03%	10	RvB Pro Forma HHI Points		**5045.2609**
	E	MSA Mean Market Share Per RvB Bank	7.10%				
	F	MSA Median Market Share for RvB Banks	4.40%		Leon L. Morris ©		

Legend	
Top 50 National Bank	
Market Share of Bank Reviewed	
Bank w. Rent v. Buy Calculator	
Calculator Performed Correctly	
Calculator Performed Incorrectly	
HHI Points	
Save in Taxes - Calculator	ST
No retail Mortgage loans solicited	NRML

Entire Houston MSA

Herfendahl-Herschman	Index	# of Institutions
Actual	1159.5376	110
Pro-Forma	5071.1348	101
Change > 100	**3911.5972**	

TABLE 44

44	State	Utah
	Metropolitan Area	Salt Lake City

Rank		Institution Name	Market Share	Rent v. Buy (RvB) Calculator	FDIC Certificate #	Calculator Performance	Actual HHI Points
1		MERRIL LYNCH BANK USA	43.09%	No	27374		1856.7481
2		UBS BANK USA	13.20%	No	57565		174.2400
3		MORGAN STANLEY BANK	7.23%	No	32992		52.2729
4		AMERICAN EXPRESS BANK FSB	6.32%	No	35328		39.9424
5	ST	ZIONS FIRST NATIONAL BANK FSB	4.40%	Yes	2270		19.3600
6		JP MORGAN CHASE BANK NA	3.17%	Yes	628		10.0489
7		WELLS FARGO BANK NA	2.62%	Yes	3511		6.8644
8		CAPMARK BANK	2.50%	NRML	57529		6.2500
9		GMAC AUTOMOTIVE BANK	2.35%	NRML	57803		5.5225
10		LEHMAN BROTHERS COML BK	2.16%	No	58009		4.6656
11		AMERICAN EXPRESS CENTURION B	1.76%	No	27471		3.0976
12		GE MONEY BANK	1.49%	No	27314		2.2201
13		BMW BANK OF NORTH AMERICA	1.27%	NRML	35141		1.6129
14		CIT BANK	1.15%	No	35575		1.3225
	A	Market Share of Banks Reviewed	92.71%	14	Banks reviewed HHI Points		2184.1679
	B	MSA Mean Market Share Per Bank Reviewed	6.62%		RvB Actual HHI Points		36.2733
	C	MSA Median Market Share Per Bank Reviewed	2.56%				
	D	Market Share of Banks with Rent v. Buy calculator	10.19%	3	RvB Pro Forma HHI Points		103.8361
	E	MSA Mean Market Share Per RvB Bank	3.40%				
	F	MSA Median Market Share for RvB Banks	3.17%		Leon L. Morris ©		

Legend	
Top 50 National Bank	
Market Share of Bank Reviewed	
Bank w. Rent v. Buy Calculator	
Calculator Performed Correctly	
Calculator Performed Incorrectly	
HHI Points	
Save in Taxes - Calculator	ST
No retail Mortgage loans solicited	NRML

Entire Salt Lake City MSA

Herfendahl-Herschman	Index	# of Institutions
Actual	2187.3316	61
Pro-Forma	2254.8862	59
Change > 100	**67.5546**	

TABLE 45

45	State	Vermont				
	Metropolitan Area	Burlington- South Burlington, VT				

Rank		Institution Name	Market Share	Rent v. Buy (RvB) Calculator	FDIC Certificate #	Calculator Performance	Actual HHI Points
1		CHITTENDEN TRUST CO	39.62%	**No**	14149		1569.7444
2		KEYBANK NATIONAL ASSN	16.72%	Yes	17534		279.5584
3		TD BANKNORTH NATIONAL ASSN	16.20%	Yes	18409		262.4400
4		MERCHANTS BANK	10.69%	**No**	6268		114.2761
5	ST	CITIZENS BANK NA	8.83%	Yes	57957		77.9689
6		PEOPLES TR CO OF ST ALBANS	4.62%	Yes	14168		21.3444
7		NORTHFIELD SAVINGS BANK	2.62%	**No**	14140		6.8644
	A	Market Share of Banks Reviewed	**99.30%**	7	Banks reviewed HHI Points		2332.1966
	B	MSA Mean Market Share Per Bank Reviewed	**14.19%**		RvB Actual HHI Points		641.3117
	C	MSA Median Market Share Per Bank Reviewed	**10.69%**				
	D	Market Share of Banks with Rent v. Buy calculator	46.37%	4	RvB Pro Forma HHI Points		**2150.1769**
	E	MSA Mean Market Share Per RvB Bank	11.59%				
	F	MSA Median Market Share for RvB Banks	12.52%		Leon L. Morris ©		

Legend	
Top 50 National Bank	
Market Share of Bank Reviewed	
Bank w. Rent v. Buy Calculator	
Calculator Performed Correctly	
Calculator Performed Incorrectly	
HHI Points	
Save in Taxes - Calculator	ST
No retail Mortgage loans solicited	NRML

Entire Burlington MSA

Herfendahl-Herschman	Index	# of Institutions
Actual	2332.7978	9
Pro-Forma	3841.7807	6
Change > 100	**1508.9829**	

TABLE 46

46	State	Virginia
	Metropolitan Area	Virginia Beach -Norfolk-Newport News, VA -NC

Rank		Institution Name	Market Share	Rent v. Buy (RvB) Calculator	FDIC Certificate #	Calculator Performance	Actual HHI Points
1		WACHOVIA BANK NATIONAL ASSN	21.38%	No	33869		457.1044
2		BRANCH B&T CO OF VIRGINIA	14.60%	Yes	22584		213.1600
3		BANK OF AMERICA NA	14.38%	Yes	3510		206.7844
4		SUNTRUST BANK	14.29%	Yes	867		204.2041
5	ST	TOWNE BANK	9.28%	Yes	35095		86.1184
6	ST	RESOURCE BANK	3.48%	Yes	27322		12.1104
7		OLD POINT NB OF PHOEBUS	3.19%	**No**	6892		10.1761
8		BANK OF THE COMMONWEALTH	2.73%	Yes	20408		7.4529
9	ST	RBC CENTURA BANK	2.23%	Yes	33184		4.9729
10		GATEWAY BANK & TRUST CO	2.09%	**No**	34861		4.3681
11		BANK OF HAMPTON ROADS	1.90%	**No**	27125		3.6100
12		MONARCH BANK	1.82%	Yes	34945		3.3124
13		FARMERS BANK	1.34%	**No**	2429		1.7956
14		CHESAPEAKE BANK	1.26%	Yes	6862		1.5876
15		HERITAGE BANK & TRUST	1.01%	**No**	22411		1.0201
	A	Market Share of Banks Reviewed	**94.98%**	15	Banks reviewed HHI Points		1217.7774
	B	MSA Mean Market Share Per Bank Reviewed	**6.33%**		RvB Actual HHI Points		739.7031
	C	MSA Median Market Share Per Bank Reviewed	**2.73%**				
	D	Market Share of Banks with Rent v. Buy calculator	64.07%	9	RvB Pro Forma HHI Points		**4104.9649**
	E	MSA Mean Market Share Per RvB Bank	7.12%				
	F	MSA Median Market Share for RvB Banks	3.48%		Leon L. Morris ©		

Legend	
Top 50 National Bank	
Market Share of Bank Reviewed	
Bank w. Rent v. Buy Calculator	
Calculator Performed Correctly	
Calculator Performed Incorrectly	
HHI Points	
Save in Taxes - Calculator	ST
No retail Mortgage loans solicited	NRML

Entire Virginia Beach MSA

Herfendahl-Herschman	Index	# of Institutions
Actual	1220.2079	33
Pro-Forma	4586.0032	25
Change > 100	**3365.7953**	

TABLE 47

47	State	Washington
	Metropolitan Area	Seattle-Tacoma-Bellevue, WA

Rank		Institution Name	Market Share	Rent v. Buy (RvB) Calculator	FDIC Certificate #	Calculator Performance	Actual HHI Points
1		BANK OF AMERICA NA	28.07%	Yes	3510		787.9249
2		WASHINGTON MUTUAL BANK	13.73%	Yes	32633		188.5129
3		U S BANK NATIONAL ASSN	13.55%	Yes	6548		183.6025
4		KEYBANK NATIONAL ASSN	9.14%	Yes	17534		83.5396
5		WELLS FARGO BANK NA	6.82%	Yes	3511		46.3761
6		FRONTIER BANK	3.28%	No	22710		10.7584
7		WASHINGTON FS&LA	2.87%	No	28088		8.2369
8		COLUMBIA STATE BANK	2.57%	No	33826		6.6049
9		HOMESTREET BANK	1.60%	Yes	32489		2.5600
10		CASCADE BANK	1.34%	Yes	28823		1.7956
11		FIRST MUTUAL BANK	1.20%	No	19835		1.4400
12		FIRST SAVINGS BANK OF RENTON	1.15%	Yes	29058		1.3225
13		CITY BANK link blocked	1.03%	No	21521		1.0609
	A	Market Share of Banks Reviewed	**86.35%**	13	Banks reviewed HHI Points		1323.7352
	B	MSA Mean Market Share Per Bank Reviewed	**6.64%**		RvB Actual HHI Points		1295.6341
	C	MSA Median Market Share Per Bank Reviewed	**2.87%**				
	D	Market Share of Banks with Rent v. Buy calculator	75.40%	8	RvB Pro Forma HHI Points		**5685.1600**
	E	MSA Mean Market Share Per RvB Bank	9.43%				
	F	MSA Median Market Share for RvB Banks	7.98%		Leon L. Morris ©		

Legend	
Top 50 National Bank	
Market Share of Bank Reviewed	
Bank w. Rent v. Buy Calculator	
Calculator Performed Correctly	
Calculator Performed Incorrectly	
HHI Points	
Save in Taxes - Calculator	ST
No retail Mortgage loans solicited	NRML

Entire Seattle MSA

Herfendahl-Herschman	Index	# of Institutions
Actual	1329.9153	76
Pro-Forma	5718.9491	69
Change > 100	**4389.034**	

TABLE 48

48	State	West Virginia
	Metropolitan Area	Charleston

Rank		Institution Name	Market Share	Rent v. Buy (RvB) Calculator	FDIC Certificate #	Calculator Performance	Actual HHI Points
1		BRANCH BANKING & TRUST CO	26.82%	Yes	9846		719.3124
2		CITY NB OF WEST VIRGINIA	11.41%	Yes	17735		130.1881
3		JP MORGAN CHASE BANK NA	10.56%	Yes	628		111.5136
4		UNITED BANK	10.22%	No	6784		104.4484
5		HUNTINGTON NATIONAL BANK	9.08%	Yes	6560		82.4464
6		PUTNAM COUNTY BANK	8.31%	No	15243		69.0561
7		SUNTRUST BANK	3.65%	Yes	867		13.3225
8		WESBANCO BANK INC	3.55%	No	803		12.6025
9		POCA VALLEY BANK INC	2.74%	No	11952		7.5076
10		BOONE COUNTY BANK INC	2.63%	No	34837		6.9169
11	ST	FIFTH THIRD BANK	2.32%	Yes	6672		5.3824
12		FIRST BANK OF CHARLESTON INC	1.94%	Y*	57514	Coming soon	3.7636
13		SUMMIT COMMUNITY BANK INC	1.27%	No	34102		1.6129
14		COMMUNITY TRUST BANK INC	1.15%	Yes	2720		1.3225
15		CLAY COUNTY BANK INC	1.14%	No	2444		1.2996
	A	Market Share of Banks Reviewed	**96.79%**	15	Banks reviewed HHI Points		1270.6955
	B	MSA Mean Market Share Per Bank Reviewed	**6.45%**		RvB Actual HHI Points		1063.4879
	C	MSA Median Market Share Per Bank Reviewed	**3.55%**				
	D	Market Share of Banks with Rent v. Buy calculator	64.99%	7	RvB Pro Forma HHI Points		**4223.7001**
	E	MSA Mean Market Share Per RvB Bank	9.28%				
	F	MSA Median Market Share for RvB Banks	9.08%		Leon L. Morris ©		
				*8/66.93%			4,479.62

Legend	
Top 50 National Bank	
Market Share of Bank Reviewed	
Bank w. Rent v. Buy Calculator	
Calculator Performed Correctly	
Calculator Performed Incorrectly	
HHI Points	
Save in Taxes - Calculator	ST
No retail Mortgage loans solicited	NRML

Entire Charleston MSA

Herfendahl-Herschman	Index	# of Institutions
Actual	1272.4727	23
Pro-Forma	4430.8412	17
Change > 100	**3158.3685**	

* coming soon - comment on what the calculator will do, but no actual calculator.

TABLE 49

49	State	Wisconsin
	Metropolitan Area	Milwaukee-Waukesha- West Allis, WI

Rank		Institution Name	Market Share	Rent v. Buy (RvB) Calculator	FDIC Certificate #	Calculator Performance	Actual HHI Points
1		M&I MARSHALL & ILSLEY BANK	28.96%	Yes	1020		838.6816
2		U S BANK NATIONAL ASSN	19.84%	Yes	6548		393.6256
3		JP MORGAN CHASE BANK NA	6.75%	Yes	628		45.5625
4	ST	ASSOCIATED BANK NA	5.51%	Yes	5296		30.3601
5		MID AMERICA BANK FSB	3.27%	Yes	28671		10.6929
6		WAUWATOSA SAVINGS BANK	2.77%	No	28513		7.6729
7		GUARANTY BANK	2.52%	Yes	30003		6.3504
8		BANK MUTUAL	2.34%	Yes	30125		5.4756
9	ST	NORTH SHORE BANK FSB	2.00%	Yes	28679		4.0000
10		PARK BANK	1.59%	Yes	26218		2.5281
11		TRI CITY NATIONAL BANK	1.52%	No	18922		2.3104
12		WELLS FARGO BANK NA	1.52%	Yes	3511		2.3104
13		OZAUKEE BANK	1.42%	Yes	22017		2.0164
14		EQUITABLE BANK SSB	1.32%	No	28614		1.7424
15		WAUKESHA STATE BANK	1.28%	No	16160		1.6384
16		CITIZENS BANK OF MUKWONAGO	1.11%	No	13055		1.2321
17		FIRST BANK FINANCIAL CENTRE	1.03%	No	12517		1.0609
	A	Market Share of Banks Reviewed	**84.75%**	17	Banks reviewed HHI Points		1357.2607
	B	MSA Mean Market Share Per Bank Reviewed	**4.99%**		RvB Actual HHI Points		1341.6036
	C	MSA Median Market Share Per Bank Reviewed	**2.00%**				
	D	Market Share of Banks with Rent v. Buy calculator	75.72%	11	RvB Pro Forma HHI Points		**5733.5184**
	E	MSA Mean Market Share Per RvB Bank	6.88%				
	F	MSA Median Market Share for RvB Banks	2.52%		Leon L. Morris ©		

Legend	
Top 50 National Bank	
Market Share of Bank Reviewed	
Bank w. Rent v. Buy Calculator	
Calculator Performed Correctly	
Calculator Performed Incorrectly	
HHI Points	
Save in Taxes - Calculator	ST
No retail Mortgage loans solicited	NRML

Entire Milwaukee MSA

Herfendahl-Herschman	Index	# of Institutions
Actual	1365.7213	65
Pro-Forma	5758.2123	55
Change > 100	**4392.4910**	

TABLE 50

50	State	Wyoming
	Metropolitan Area	Cheyenne, WY

Rank		Institution Name	Market Share	Rent v. Buy (RvB) Calculator	FDIC Certificate #	Calculator Performance	Actual HHI Points
1		U S BANK NATIONAL ASSN	23.83%	Yes	6548		567.8689
2		AMERICAN NATIONAL BANK	12.67%	Yes	19220		160.5289
3	ST	BANK OF THE WEST	11.35%	Yes	3514		128.8225
4		WELLS FARGO BANK NA	11.33%	Yes	3511		128.3689
5		FIRST INTERSTATE BANK	9.73%	Yes	1105		94.6729
6		WYOMING BANK & TRUST	6.30%	**No**	8718		39.6900
7		WESTERN BANK OF CHEYENNE	5.94%	**No**	25154		35.2836
8		FIRST NB OF WYOMING	5.14%	**No**	19266		26.4196
9		SECURITY FIRST BANK	3.67%	Yes	31966		13.4689
10		TRI-COUNTY NATIONAL BANK	2.52%	**No**	29608		6.3504
11		CHEYENNE STATE BANK	2.38%	**No**	57363		5.6644
12		PINNACLE BANK WYOMING	1.71%	**No**	2232		2.9241
13		FIRSTIER BANK WYOMING	1.15%	**No**	522		1.3225
14		FIRST NB OF SIDNEY	1.07%	**No**	25127		1.1449
15		FARMERS STATE BANK	1.03%	No Website	526		1.0609
	A	Market Share of Banks Reviewed	**99.82%**	15	Banks reviewed HHI Points		1213.5914
	B	MSA Mean Market Share Per Bank Reviewed	**6.65%**		RvB Actual HHI Points		1093.7310
	C	MSA Median Market Share Per Bank Reviewed	**3.67%**				
	D	Market Share of Banks with Rent v. Buy calculator	72.58%	6	RvB Pro Forma HHI Points		**5267.8564**
	E	MSA Mean Market Share Per RvB Bank	12.10%				
	F	MSA Median Market Share for RvB Banks	11.34%		Leon L. Morris ©		

Legend	
Top 50 National Bank	
Market Share of Bank Reviewed	
Bank w. Rent v. Buy Calculator	
Calculator Performed Correctly	
Calculator Performed Incorrectly	
HHI Points	
Save in Taxes - Calculator	ST
No retail Mortgage loans solicited	NRML

Entire Cheyenne MSA

Herfendahl-Herschman	Index	# of Institutions
Actual	1213.6203	17
Pro-Forma	5387.7457	13
Change > 100	**4174.1254**	

APPENDIX B

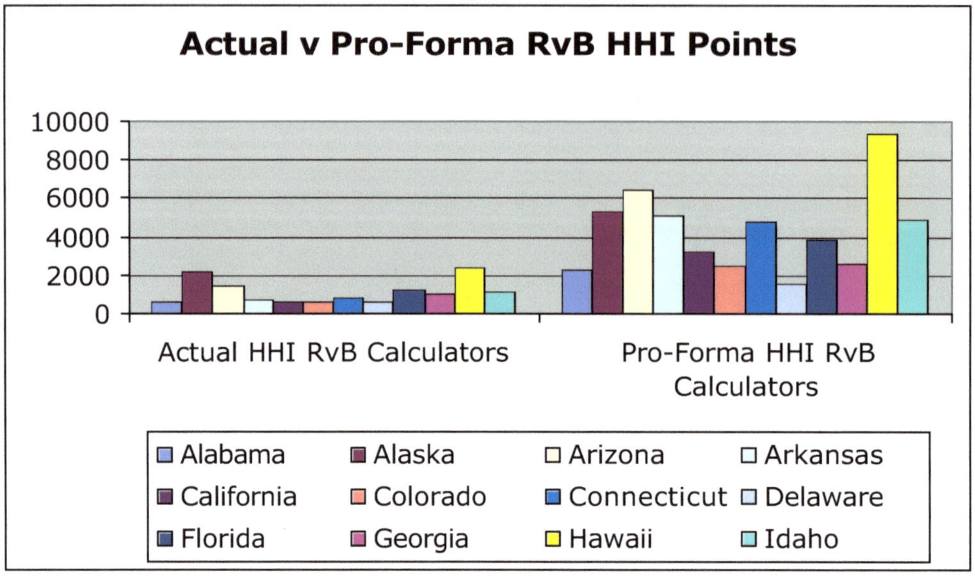

Note: The actual and pro-forma HHI for each MSAs is indicated by State. (2 of 4)

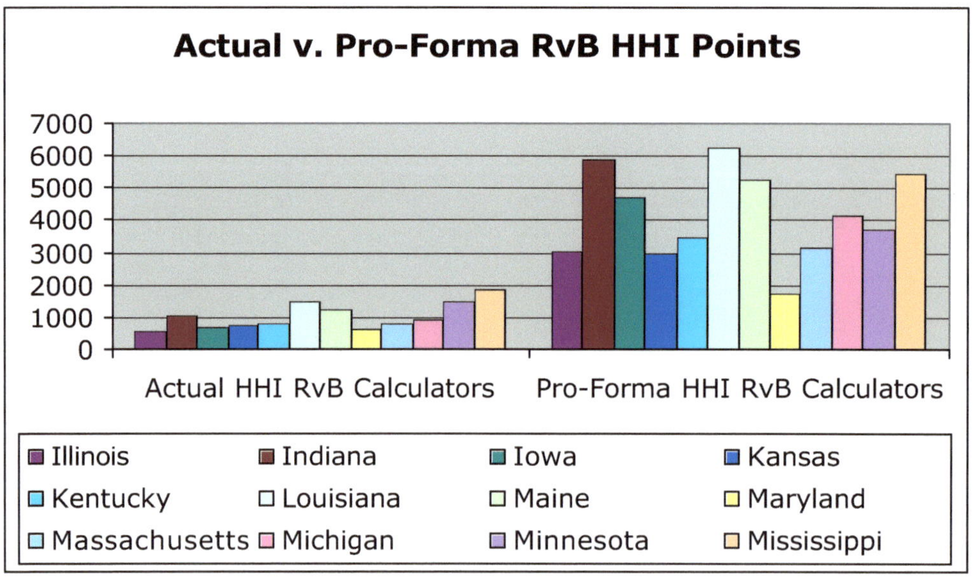

Note: The actual and pro-forma HHI for each MSAs is indicated by State. (3 of 4)

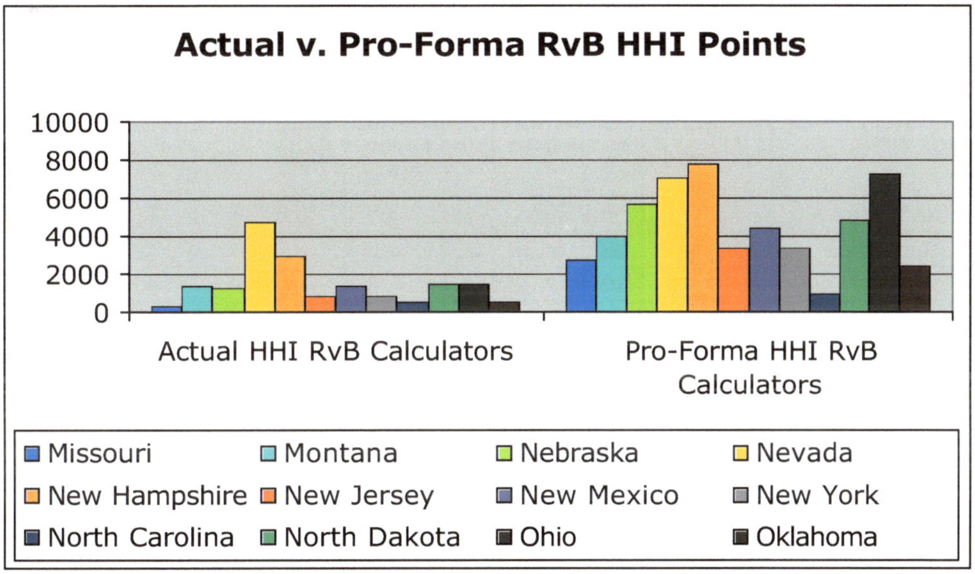

Note: The actual and pro-forma HHI for each MSAs is indicated by State. (4 of 4)

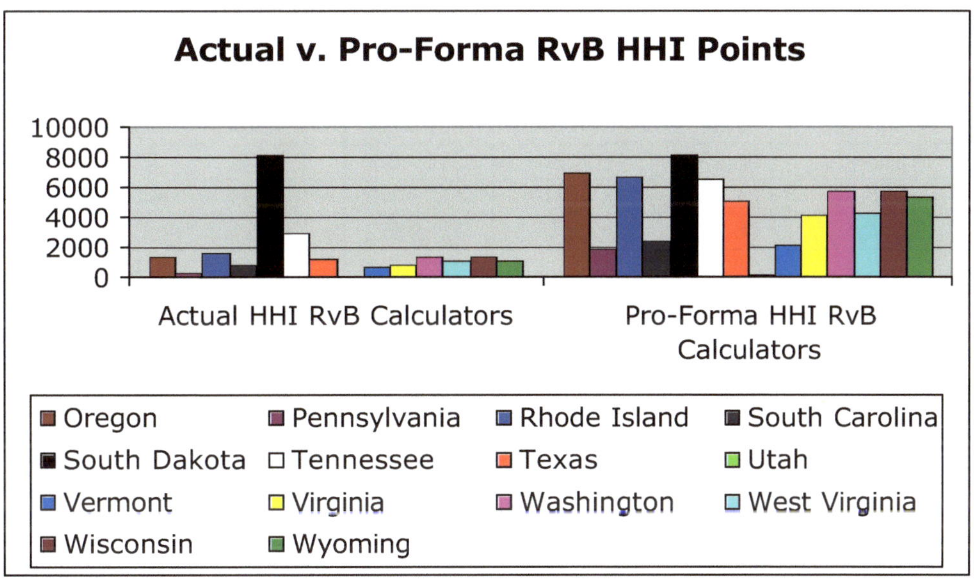

Table 1

Legend: Summary Data Listed Alphabetically by State (Part One).

	State	MSA	Market Share of Institutions Reviewed	Actual HHI Entire MSA	Actual HH Index Banks Reviewed 1%ers	HHI Point Difference MSA v 1%'s	Market Share of Institutions w/ RvB	Actual HHI RvB Calculators
1	Alabama	Birmingham	88.56%	969.6851	963.0066	6.6785	47.47%	636.5385
2	Alaska	Anchorage	99.99%	2875.8136	2875.4431	0.3705	72.92%	2209.6602
3	Arizona	Phoenix	89.12%	1509.8192	1505.701	4.1182	80.45%	1480.2103
4	Arkansas	Little Rock	93.30%	786.8591	782.1736	4.6855	71.75%	714.7287
5	California	Los Angeles	79.35%	741.8627	732.6973	9.1654	56.65%	668.0541
6	Colorado	Denver	77.83%	734.7589	722.7543	12.0046	49.61%	607.8427
7	Connecticut	Bridgeport	95.10%	1109.3498	1106.2928	3.0570	69.41%	832.9339
8	Delaware	Wilmington	95.69%	1741.9743	1740.2407	1.7336	39.82%	632.2762
9	Florida	Jacksonville	90.76%	1929.4173	1924.8795	4.5378	61.75%	1275.3315
10	Georgia	Atlanta	75.84%	1411.9399	1403.6294	8.3105	51.45%	1018.1935
11	Hawaii	Honolulu	98.73%	2411.9706	2411.9705	0.0001	97.00%	2408.9776
12	Idaho	Boise	97.28%	1240.9446	1238.93	2.0146	69.80%	1109.9522
13	Illinois	Chicago	66.25%	599.0443	588.5273	10.5170	55.06%	563.5726
14	Indiana	Indianapolis	88.34%	1123.658	1116.92	6.7380	76.80%	1068.2162
15	Iowa	Des Moines	85.60%	759.3428	749.9186	9.4242	68.48%	652.5998
16	Kansas	Wichita	83.47%	936.2305	927.2679	8.9626	54.70%	752.272
17	Kentucky	Lexington	93.43%	781.4255	776.9679	4.4576	58.74%	776.9679
18	Louisiana	New Orleans	92.64%	1539.3939	1535.9908	3.4031	79.09%	1513.2575
19	Maine	Portland	96.23%	1309.0473	1306.4065	2.6408	72.55%	1222.7809
20	Maryland	Baltimore	81.33%	934.2498	924.8045	9.4453	41.73%	647.6083
21	Massachusetts	Boston	76.94%	909.7003	901.9352	7.7651	56.40%	777.6326
22	Michigan	Detroit	88.39%	1426.9336	1421.4859	5.4477	64.47%	900.3915
23	Minnesota	Minneapolis	70.19%	1565.8816	1555.3019	10.5797	61.09%	1507.6311
24	Mississippi	Jackson	95.65%	1971.004	1968.5299	2.4741	74.02%	1865.7394
25	Missouri	Kansas City	68.63%	408.4852	394.7811	13.7041	51.93%	354.5459

Table 2

Legend: Summary Data Listed Alphabetically by State (Part Two)

	State	MSA	Market Share of Institutions Reviewed	Actual HHI Entire MSA	Actual HH Index Banks Reviewed 1%ers	HHI Point Difference MSA v 1%'s	Market Share of Institutions w/ RvB	Actual HHI RvB Calculators
26	Montana	Billings	99.81%	1613.6276	1613.5915	0.0361	63.38%	1352.974
27	Nebraska	Omaha	84.83%	1335.2406	1328.6897	6.5509	75.31%	1307.9029
28	Nevada	Las Vegas	92.24%	4770.0908	4765.2452	4.8456	83.89%	4721.7727
29	New Hampshire	Manchester	97.96%	3023.7918	3022.9252	0.8666	87.98%	2986.983
30	New Jersey	Newark	81.29%	1105.8306	1099.5491	6.2815	57.67%	824.4529
31	New Mexico	Albuquerque	95.78%	1659.5141	1656.6846	2.8295	66.37%	1327.1815
32	New York	New York	81.29%	1105.8306	1099.5491	6.2815	57.67%	824.4529
33	North Carolina	Charlotte	94.87%	4625.7012	4623.1877	2.5135	31.06%	551.4716
34	North Dakota	Fargo	94.59%	1571.9141	1568.5483	3.3658	69.27%	1461.2681
35	Ohio	Columbus	90.37%	1490.3248	1485.8463	4.4785	85.06%	1478.4278
36	Oklahoma	Oklahoma City	81.24%	675.4735	664.2818	11.1917	49.18%	551.0374
37	Oregon	Portland	91.03%	1330.7678	1325.7025	5.0653	83.16%	1308.652
38	Pennsylvania	Philadelphia	80.97%	786.3196	779.2625	7.0571	43.90%	319.3636
39	Rhode Island	Providence	93.97%	1613.9869	1611.3269	2.6600	81.95%	1584.6627
40	South Carolina	Columbia	94.36%	1470.5946	1467.6462	2.9484	49.53%	734.5777
41	South Dakota	Sioux Falls	94.09%	8145.2937	8142.4683	2.8254	90.19%	8134.2361
42	Tennessee	Memphis	86.25%	2959.9872	2953.0785	6.9087	81.23%	2938.1021
43	Texas	Houston	81.83%	1159.5376	1151.3547	8.1829	71.03%	1133.8195
44	Utah	Salt Lake City	92.71%	2187.3316	2184.1679	3.1637	10.19%	36.2733
45	Vermont	Burlington	99.30%	2332.7978	2332.1966	0.6012	46.37%	641.3117
46	Virginia	Virginia Beach	94.98%	1220.2079	1217.7774	2.4305	64.07%	739.7031
47	Washington	Seattle	86.35%	1329.9153	1323.7352	6.1801	75.40%	1295.6341
48	West Virginia	Charleston	96.79%	1272.4727	1270.6955	1.7772	64.99%	1063.4879
49	Wisconsin	Milwaukee	84.75%	1365.7213	1357.2607	8.4606	75.72%	1341.6036
50	Wyoming	Cheyenne	99.82%	1213.6203	1213.5914	0.0289	72.58%	1093.731

Table 3:

Legend: Listed by Market Share, Lowest - Highest 1%ers (Part One)

	State	MSA	Market Share of Institutions Reviewed	Actual HHI Entire MSA	Actual HH Index Banks Reviewed 1%ers	HHI Point Difference MSA v 1%'s	Market Share of Institutions w/ RvB	Actual HHI RvB Calculators
1	Illinois	Chicago	66.25%	599.0443	588.5273	10.5170	55.06%	563.5726
2	Missouri	Kansas City	68.63%	408.4852	394.7811	13.7041	51.93%	354.5459
3	Minnesota	Minneapolis	70.19%	1565.8816	1555.3019	10.5797	61.09%	1507.6311
4	Georgia	Atlanta	75.84%	1411.9399	1403.6294	8.3105	51.45%	1018.1935
5	Massachusetts	Boston	76.94%	909.7003	901.9352	7.7651	56.40%	777.6326
6	Colorado	Denver	77.83%	734.7589	722.7543	12.0046	49.61%	607.8427
7	California	Los Angeles	79.35%	741.8627	732.6973	9.1654	56.65%	668.0541
8	Pennsylvania	Philadelphia	80.97%	786.3196	779.2625	7.0571	43.90%	319.3636
9	Oklahoma	Oklahoma City	81.24%	675.4735	664.2818	11.1917	49.18%	551.0374
10	New Jersey	Newark	81.29%	1105.8306	1099.5491	6.2815	57.67%	824.4529
11	New York	New York	81.29%	1105.8306	1099.5491	6.2815	57.67%	824.4529
12	Maryland	Baltimore	81.33%	934.2498	924.8045	9.4453	41.73%	647.6083
13	Texas	Houston	81.83%	1159.5376	1151.3547	8.1829	71.03%	1133.8195
14	Kansas	Wichita	83.47%	936.2305	927.2679	8.9626	54.70%	752.272
15	Wisconsin	Milwaukee	84.75%	1365.7213	1357.2607	8.4606	75.72%	1341.6036
16	Nebraska	Omaha	84.83%	1335.2406	1328.6897	6.5509	75.31%	1307.9029
17	Iowa	Des Moines	85.60%	759.3428	749.9186	9.4242	68.48%	652.5998
18	Tennessee	Memphis	86.25%	2959.9872	2953.0785	6.9087	81.23%	2938.1021
19	Washington	Seattle	86.35%	1329.9153	1323.7352	6.1801	75.40%	1295.6341
20	Indiana	Indianapolis	88.34%	1123.658	1116.92	6.7380	76.80%	1068.2162
21	Michigan	Detroit	88.39%	1426.9336	1421.4859	5.4477	64.47%	900.3915
22	Alabama	Birmingham	88.56%	969.6851	963.0066	6.6785	47.47%	636.5385
23	Arizona	Phoenix	89.12%	1509.8192	1505.701	4.1182	80.45%	1480.2103
24	Ohio	Columbus	90.37%	1490.3248	1485.8463	4.4785	85.06%	1478.4278
25	Florida	Jacksonville	90.76%	1929.4173	1924.8795	4.5378	61.75%	1275.3315

Table 4:

Legend: Listed by Market Share, Lowest - Highest 1%ers (Part Two)

	State	MSA	Market Share of Institutions Reviewed	Actual HHI Entire MSA	Actual HH Index Banks Reviewed 1%ers	HHI Point Difference MSA v 1%ers	Market Share of Institutions w/ RvB	Actual HHI RvB Calculators
26	Oregon	Portland	91.03%	1330.7678	1325.7025	5.0653	83.16%	1308.652
27	Nevada	Las Vegas	92.24%	4770.0908	4765.2452	4.8456	83.89%	4721.7727
28	Louisiana	New Orleans	92.64%	1539.3939	1535.9908	3.4031	79.09%	1513.2575
29	Utah	Salt Lake City	92.71%	2187.3316	2184.1679	3.1637	10.19%	36.2733
30	Arkansas	Little Rock	93.30%	786.8591	782.1736	4.6855	71.75%	714.7287
31	Kentucky	Lexington	93.43%	781.4255	776.9679	4.4576	58.74%	776.9679
32	Rhode Island	Providence	93.97%	1613.9869	1611.3269	2.6600	81.95%	1584.6627
33	South Dakota	Sioux Falls	94.09%	8145.2937	8142.4683	2.8254	90.19%	8134.2361
34	South Carolina	Columbia	94.36%	1470.5946	1467.6462	2.9484	49.53%	734.5777
35	North Dakota	Fargo	94.59%	1571.9141	1568.5483	3.3658	69.27%	1461.2681
36	North Carolina	Charlotte	94.87%	4625.7012	4623.1877	2.5135	31.06%	551.4716
37	Virginia	Virginia Beach	94.98%	1220.2079	1217.7774	2.4305	64.07%	739.7031
38	Connecticut	Bridgeport	95.10%	1109.3498	1106.2928	3.0570	69.41%	832.9339
39	Mississippi	Jackson	95.65%	1971.004	1968.5299	2.4741	74.02%	1865.7394
40	Delaware	Wilmington	95.69%	1741.9743	1740.2407	1.7336	39.82%	632.2762
41	New Mexico	Albuquerque	95.78%	1659.5141	1656.6846	2.8295	66.37%	1327.1815
42	Maine	Portland	96.23%	1309.0473	1306.4065	2.6408	72.55%	1222.7809
43	West Virginia	Charleston	96.79%	1272.4727	1270.6955	1.7772	64.99%	1063.4879
44	Idaho	Boise	97.28%	1240.9446	1238.93	2.0146	69.80%	1109.9522
45	New Hampshire	Manchester	97.96%	3023.7918	3022.9252	0.8666	87.98%	2986.983
46	Hawaii	Honolulu	98.73%	2411.9706	2411.9705	0.0001	97.00%	2408.9776
47	Vermont	Burlington	99.30%	2332.7978	2332.1966	0.6012	46.37%	641.3117
48	Montana	Billings	99.81%	1613.6276	1613.5915	0.0361	63.38%	1352.974
49	Wyoming	Cheyenne	99.82%	1213.6203	1213.5914	0.0289	72.58%	1093.731
50	Alaska	Anchorage	99.99%	2875.8136	2875.4431	0.3705	72.92%	2209.6602

Table 5:

Legend: Ranked by Actual HHI for the MSA (lowest to highest) (Part One)

	State	MSA	Market Share of Institutions Reviewed	Actual HHI Entire MSA	Actual HH Index Banks Reviewed 1%ers	HHI Point Difference MSA v 1%ers	Market Share of Institutions w/ RvB	Actual HHI RvB Calculators	
1	Missouri	Kansas City	68.63%	408.4852	394.7811	13.7041	51.93%	354.5459	Low Market Concentration
2	Illinois	Chicago	66.25%	599.0443	588.5273	10.5170	55.06%	563.5726	
3	Oklahoma	Oklahoma City	81.24%	675.4735	664.2818	11.1917	49.18%	551.0374	
4	Colorado	Denver	77.83%	734.7589	722.7543	12.0046	49.61%	607.8427	
5	California	Los Angeles	79.35%	741.8627	732.6973	9.1654	56.65%	668.0541	
6	Iowa	Des Moines	85.60%	759.3428	749.9186	9.4242	68.48%	652.5998	
7	Kentucky	Lexington	93.43%	781.4255	776.9679	4.4576	58.74%	776.9679	
8	Pennsylvania	Philadelphia	80.97%	786.3196	779.2625	7.0571	43.90%	319.3636	
9	Arkansas	Little Rock	93.30%	786.8591	782.1736	4.6855	71.75%	714.7287	
10	Massachusetts	Boston	76.94%	909.7003	901.9352	7.7651	56.40%	777.6326	
11	Maryland	Baltimore	81.33%	934.2498	924.8045	9.4453	41.73%	647.6083	
12	Kansas	Wichita	83.47%	936.2305	927.2679	8.9626	54.70%	752.272	
13	Alabama	Birmingham	88.56%	969.6851	963.0066	6.6785	47.47%	636.5385	
14	New Jersey	Newark	81.29%	1105.8306	1099.5491	6.2815	57.67%	824.4529	Moderate Market Concentration
15	New York	New York	81.29%	1105.8306	1099.5491	6.2815	57.67%	824.4529	
16	Connecticut	Bridgeport	95.10%	1109.3498	1106.2928	3.0570	69.41%	832.9339	
17	Indiana	Indianapolis	88.34%	1123.658	1116.92	6.7380	76.80%	1068.2162	
18	Texas	Houston	81.83%	1159.5376	1151.3547	8.1829	71.03%	1133.8195	
19	Wyoming	Cheyenne	99.82%	1213.6203	1213.5914	0.0289	72.58%	1093.731	
20	Virginia	Virginia Beach	94.98%	1220.2079	1217.7774	2.4305	64.07%	739.7031	
21	Idaho	Boise	97.28%	1240.9446	1238.93	2.0146	69.80%	1109.9522	
22	West Virginia	Charleston	96.79%	1272.4727	1270.6955	1.7772	64.99%	1063.4879	
23	Maine	Portland	96.23%	1309.0473	1306.4065	2.6408	72.55%	1222.7809	
24	Washington	Seattle	86.35%	1329.9153	1323.7352	6.1801	75.40%	1295.6341	
25	Oregon	Portland	91.03%	1330.7678	1325.7025	5.0653	83.16%	1308.652	

Table 6:

Legend: Ranked by Actual HHI for the MSA (lowest to highest) (Part Two)

	State	MSA	Market Share of Institutions Reviewed	Actual HHI Entire MSA	Actual HH Index Banks Reviewed 1%ers	HHI Point Difference MSA v 1%ers	Market Share of Institutions w/ RvB	Actual HHI RvB Calculators
26	Nebraska	Omaha	84.83%	1335.2406	1328.6897	6.5509	75.31%	1307.9029
27	Wisconsin	Milwaukee	84.75%	1365.7213	1357.2607	8.4606	75.72%	1341.6036
28	Georgia	Atlanta	75.84%	1411.9399	1403.6294	8.3105	51.45%	1018.1935
29	Michigan	Detroit	88.39%	1426.9336	1421.4859	5.4477	64.47%	900.3915
30	South Carolina	Columbia	94.36%	1470.5946	1467.6462	2.9484	49.53%	734.5777
31	Ohio	Columbus	90.37%	1490.3248	1485.8463	4.4785	85.06%	1478.4278
32	Arizona	Phoenix	89.12%	1509.8192	1505.701	4.1182	80.45%	1480.2103
33	Louisiana	New Orleans	92.64%	1539.3939	1535.9908	3.4031	79.09%	1513.2575
34	Minnesota	Minneapolis	70.19%	1565.8816	1555.3019	10.5797	61.09%	1507.6311
35	North Dakota	Fargo	94.59%	1571.9141	1568.5483	3.3658	69.27%	1461.2681
36	Montana	Billings	99.81%	1613.6276	1613.5915	0.0361	63.38%	1352.974
37	Rhode Island	Providence	93.97%	1613.9869	1611.3269	2.6600	81.95%	1584.6627
38	New Mexico	Albuquerque	95.78%	1659.5141	1656.6846	2.8295	66.37%	1327.1815
39	Delaware	Wilmington	95.69%	1741.9743	1740.2407	1.7336	39.82%	632.2762
40	Florida	Jacksonville	90.76%	1929.4173	1924.8795	4.5378	61.75%	1275.3315
41	Mississippi	Jackson	95.65%	1971.004	1968.5299	2.4741	74.02%	1865.7394
42	Utah	Salt Lake City	92.71%	2187.3316	2184.1679	3.1637	10.19%	36.2733
43	Vermont	Burlington	99.30%	2332.7978	2332.1966	0.6012	46.37%	641.3117
44	Hawaii	Honolulu	98.73%	2411.9706	2411.9705	0.0001	97.00%	2408.9776
45	Alaska	Anchorage	99.99%	2875.8136	2875.4431	0.3705	72.92%	2209.6602
46	Tennessee	Memphis	86.25%	2959.9872	2953.0785	6.9087	81.23%	2938.1021
47	New Hampshire	Manchester	97.96%	3023.7918	3022.9252	0.8666	87.98%	2986.983
48	North Carolina	Charlotte	94.87%	4625.7012	4623.1877	2.5135	31.06%	551.4716
49	Nevada	Las Vegas	92.24%	4770.0908	4765.2452	4.8456	83.89%	4721.7727
50	South Dakota	Sioux Falls	94.09%	8145.2937	8142.4683	2.8254	90.19%	8134.2361

Moderate Market Concentration

Highly Concentrated Market

Table 7:

Legend: Ranked by Actual HHI for banks Reviewed (1%ers) (lowest to highest) (Part One)

	State	MSA	Market Share of Institutions Reviewed	Actual HHI Entire MSA	Actual HH Index Banks Reviewed 1%ers	HHI Point Difference MSA v 1%ers	Market Share of Institutions w/ RvB	Actual HHI RvB Calculators
1	Missouri	Kansas City	68.63%	408.4852	394.7811	13.7041	51.93%	354.5459
2	Illinois	Chicago	66.25%	599.0443	588.5273	10.5170	55.06%	563.5726
3	Oklahoma	Oklahoma City	81.24%	675.4735	664.2818	11.1917	49.18%	551.0374
4	Colorado	Denver	77.83%	734.7589	722.7543	12.0046	49.61%	607.8427
5	California	Los Angeles	79.35%	741.8627	732.6973	9.1654	56.65%	668.0541
6	Iowa	Des Moines	85.60%	759.3428	749.9186	9.4242	68.48%	652.5998
7	Kentucky	Lexington	93.43%	781.4255	776.9679	4.4576	58.74%	776.9679
8	Pennsylvania	Philadelphia	80.97%	786.3196	779.2625	7.0571	43.90%	319.3636
9	Arkansas	Little Rock	93.30%	786.8591	782.1736	4.6855	71.75%	714.7287
10	Massachusetts	Boston	76.94%	909.7003	901.9352	7.7651	56.40%	777.6326
11	Maryland	Baltimore	81.33%	934.2498	924.8045	9.4453	41.73%	647.6083
12	Kansas	Wichita	83.47%	936.2305	927.2679	8.9626	54.70%	752.272
13	Alabama	Birmingham	88.56%	969.6851	963.0066	6.6785	47.47%	636.5385
14	New Jersey	Newark	81.29%	1105.8306	1099.5491	6.2815	57.67%	824.4529
15	New York	New York	81.29%	1105.8306	1099.5491	6.2815	57.67%	824.4529
16	Connecticut	Bridgeport	95.10%	1109.3498	1106.2928	3.0570	69.41%	832.9339
17	Indiana	Indianapolis	88.34%	1123.658	1116.92	6.7380	76.80%	1068.2162
18	Texas	Houston	81.83%	1159.5376	1151.3547	8.1829	71.03%	1133.8195
19	Wyoming	Cheyenne	99.82%	1213.6203	1213.5914	0.0289	72.58%	1093.731
20	Virginia	Virginia Beach	94.98%	1220.2079	1217.7774	2.4305	64.07%	739.7031
21	Idaho	Boise	97.28%	1240.9446	1238.93	2.0146	69.80%	1109.9522
22	West Virginia	Charleston	96.79%	1272.4727	1270.6955	1.7772	64.99%	1063.4879
23	Maine	Portland	96.23%	1309.0473	1306.4065	2.6408	72.55%	1222.7809
24	Washington	Seattle	86.35%	1329.9153	1323.7352	6.1801	75.40%	1295.6341
25	Oregon	Portland	91.03%	1330.7678	1325.7025	5.0653	83.16%	1308.652

Table 8:

Legend: Ranked by Actual HHI for banks Reviewed (1%ers) (lowest to highest) (Part Two)

	State	MSA	Market Share of Institutions Reviewed	Actual HHI Entire MSA	Actual HH Index Banks Reviewed 1%ers	HHI Point Difference MSA v 1%ers	Market Share of Institutions w/ RvB	Actual HHI RvB Calculators
26	Nebraska	Omaha	84.83%	1335.2406	1328.6897	6.5509	75.31%	1307.9029
27	Wisconsin	Milwaukee	84.75%	1365.7213	1357.2607	8.4606	75.72%	1341.6036
28	Georgia	Atlanta	75.84%	1411.9399	1403.6294	8.3105	51.45%	1018.1935
29	Michigan	Detroit	88.39%	1426.9336	1421.4859	5.4477	64.47%	900.3915
30	South Carolina	Columbia	94.36%	1470.5946	1467.6462	2.9484	49.53%	734.5777
31	Ohio	Columbus	90.37%	1490.3248	1485.8463	4.4785	85.06%	1478.4278
32	Arizona	Phoenix	89.12%	1509.8192	1505.701	4.1182	80.45%	1480.2103
33	Louisiana	New Orleans	92.64%	1539.3939	1535.9908	3.4031	79.09%	1513.2575
34	Minnesota	Minneapolis	70.19%	1565.8816	1555.3019	10.5797	61.09%	1507.6311
35	North Dakota	Fargo	94.59%	1571.9141	1568.5483	3.3658	69.27%	1461.2681
36	Rhode Island	Providence	93.97%	1613.9869	1611.3269	2.6600	81.95%	1584.6627
37	Montana	Billings	99.81%	1613.6276	1613.5915	0.0361	63.38%	1352.974
38	New Mexico	Albuquerque	95.78%	1659.5141	1656.6846	2.8295	66.37%	1327.1815
39	Delaware	Wilmington	95.69%	1741.9743	1740.2407	1.7336	39.82%	632.2762
40	Florida	Jacksonville	90.76%	1929.4173	1924.8795	4.5378	61.75%	1275.3315
41	Mississippi	Jackson	95.65%	1971.004	1968.5299	2.4741	74.02%	1865.7394
42	Utah	Salt Lake City	92.71%	2187.3316	2184.1679	3.1637	10.19%	36.2733
43	Vermont	Burlington	99.30%	2332.7978	2332.1966	0.6012	46.37%	641.3117
44	Hawaii	Honolulu	98.73%	2411.9706	2411.9705	0.0001	97.00%	2408.9776
45	Alaska	Anchorage	99.99%	2875.8136	2875.4431	0.3705	72.92%	2209.6602
46	Tennessee	Memphis	86.25%	2959.9872	2953.0785	6.9087	81.23%	2938.1021
47	New Hampshire	Manchester	97.96%	3023.7918	3022.9252	0.8666	87.98%	2986.983
48	North Carolina	Charlotte	94.87%	4625.7012	4623.1877	2.5135	31.06%	551.4716
49	Nevada	Las Vegas	92.24%	4770.0908	4765.2452	4.8456	83.89%	4721.7727
50	South Dakota	Sioux Falls	94.09%	8145.2937	8142.4683	2.8254	90.19%	8134.2361

Table 9:

Legend: Ranked by Actual HHI Point Difference - MSA & Banks Reviewed (1%ers) (lowest to highest)

	State	MSA	Market Share of Institutions Reviewed	Actual HHI Entire MSA	Actual HH Index Banks Reviewed 1%ers	HHI Point Difference MSA v 1%ers	Market Share of Institutions w/ RvB	Actual HHI RvB Calculators
1	Hawaii	Honolulu	98.73%	2411.9706	2411.9705	0.0001	97.00%	2408.9776
2	Wyoming	Cheyenne	99.82%	1213.6203	1213.5914	0.0289	72.58%	1093.731
3	Montana	Billings	99.81%	1613.6276	1613.5915	0.0361	63.38%	1352.974
4	Alaska	Anchorage	99.99%	2875.8136	2875.4431	0.3705	72.92%	2209.6602
5	Vermont	Burlington	99.30%	2332.7978	2332.1966	0.6012	46.37%	641.3117
6	New Hampshire	Manchester	97.96%	3023.7918	3022.9252	0.8666	87.98%	2986.983
7	Delaware	Wilmington	95.69%	1741.9743	1740.2407	1.7336	39.82%	632.2762
8	West Virginia	Charleston	96.79%	1272.4727	1270.6955	1.7772	64.99%	1063.4879
9	Idaho	Boise	97.28%	1240.9446	1238.93	2.0146	69.80%	1109.9522
10	Virginia	Virginia Beach	94.98%	1220.2079	1217.7774	2.4305	64.07%	739.7031
11	Mississippi	Jackson	95.65%	1971.004	1968.5299	2.4741	74.02%	1865.7394
12	North Carolina	Charlotte	94.87%	4625.7012	4623.1877	2.5135	31.06%	551.4716
13	Maine	Portland	96.23%	1309.0473	1306.4065	2.6408	72.55%	1222.7809
14	Rhode Island	Providence	93.97%	1613.9869	1611.3269	2.6600	81.95%	1584.6627
15	South Dakota	Sioux Falls	94.09%	8145.2937	8142.4683	2.8254	90.19%	8134.2361
16	New Mexico	Albuquerque	95.78%	1659.5141	1656.6846	2.8295	66.37%	1327.1815
17	South Carolina	Columbia	94.36%	1470.5946	1467.6462	2.9484	49.53%	734.5777
18	Connecticut	Bridgeport	95.10%	1109.3498	1106.2928	3.0570	69.41%	832.9339
19	Utah	Salt Lake City	92.71%	2187.3316	2184.1679	3.1637	10.19%	36.2733
20	North Dakota	Fargo	94.59%	1571.9141	1568.5483	3.3658	69.27%	1461.2681
21	Louisiana	New Orleans	92.64%	1539.3939	1535.9908	3.4031	79.09%	1513.2575
22	Arizona	Phoenix	89.12%	1509.8192	1505.701	4.1182	80.45%	1480.2103
23	Kentucky	Lexington	93.43%	781.4255	776.9679	4.4576	58.74%	776.9679
24	Ohio	Columbus	90.37%	1490.3248	1485.8463	4.4785	85.06%	1478.4278
25	Florida	Jacksonville	90.76%	1929.4173	1924.8795	4.5378	61.75%	1275.3315

Table 10:

Legend: Ranked by Actual HHI Point Difference - MSA & Banks Reviewed (1%ers) (lowest to highest) (Pt 2)

	State	MSA	Market Share of Institutions Reviewed	Actual HHI Entire MSA	Actual HH Index Banks Reviewed 1%ers	HHI Point Difference MSA v 1%ers	Market Share of Institutions w/ RvB	Actual HHI RvB Calculators
26	Arkansas	Little Rock	93.30%	786.8591	782.1736	4.6855	71.75%	714.7287
27	Nevada	Las Vegas	92.24%	4770.0908	4765.2452	4.8456	83.89%	4721.7727
28	Oregon	Portland	91.03%	1330.7678	1325.7025	5.0653	83.16%	1308.652
29	Michigan	Detroit	88.39%	1426.9336	1421.4859	5.4477	64.47%	900.3915
30	Washington	Seattle	86.35%	1329.9153	1323.7352	6.1801	75.40%	1295.6341
31	New Jersey	Newark	81.29%	1105.8306	1099.5491	6.2815	57.67%	824.4529
32	New York	New York	81.29%	1105.8306	1099.5491	6.2815	57.67%	824.4529
33	Nebraska	Omaha	84.83%	1335.2406	1328.6897	6.5509	75.31%	1307.9029
34	Alabama	Birmingham	88.56%	969.6851	963.0066	6.6785	47.47%	636.5385
35	Indiana	Indianapolis	88.34%	1123.658	1116.92	6.7380	76.80%	1068.2162
36	Tennessee	Memphis	86.25%	2959.9872	2953.0785	6.9087	81.23%	2938.1021
37	Pennsylvania	Philadelphia	80.97%	786.3196	779.2625	7.0571	43.90%	319.3636
38	Massachusetts	Boston	76.94%	909.7003	901.9352	7.7651	56.40%	777.6326
39	Texas	Houston	81.83%	1159.5376	1151.3547	8.1829	71.03%	1133.8195
40	Georgia	Atlanta	75.84%	1411.9399	1403.6294	8.3105	51.45%	1018.1935
41	Wisconsin	Milwaukee	84.75%	1365.7213	1357.2607	8.4606	75.72%	1341.6036
42	Kansas	Wichita	83.47%	936.2305	927.2679	8.9626	54.70%	752.272
43	California	Los Angeles	79.35%	741.8627	732.6973	9.1654	56.65%	668.0541
44	Iowa	Des Moines	85.60%	759.3428	749.9186	9.4242	68.48%	652.5998
45	Maryland	Baltimore	81.33%	934.2498	924.8045	9.4453	41.73%	647.6083
46	Illinois	Chicago	66.25%	599.0443	588.5273	10.5170	55.06%	563.5726
47	Minnesota	Minneapolis	70.19%	1565.8816	1555.3019	10.5797	61.09%	1507.6311
48	Oklahoma	Oklahoma City	81.24%	675.4735	664.2818	11.1917	49.18%	551.0374
49	Colorado	Denver	77.83%	734.7589	722.7543	12.0046	49.61%	607.8427
50	Missouri	Kansas City	68.63%	408.4852	394.7811	13.7041	51.93%	354.5459

Table 11:

Legend: Ranked by Market Share of Banks w/ RvB Calculators (lowest to highest) (Part One)

	State	MSA	Market Share of Institutions Reviewed	Actual HHI Entire MSA	Actual HH Index Banks Reviewed 1%ers	HHI Point Difference MSA v 1%ers	Market Share of Institutions w/ RvB	Actual HHI RvB Calculators
1	Utah	Salt Lake City	92.71%	2187.3316	2184.1679	3.1637	10.19%	36.2733
2	North Carolina	Charlotte	94.87%	4625.7012	4623.1877	2.5135	31.06%	551.4716
3	Delaware	Wilmington	95.69%	1741.9743	1740.2407	1.7336	39.82%	632.2762
4	Maryland	Baltimore	81.33%	934.2498	924.8045	9.4453	41.73%	647.6083
5	Pennsylvania	Philadelphia	80.97%	786.3196	779.2625	7.0571	43.90%	319.3636
6	Vermont	Burlington	99.30%	2332.7978	2332.1966	0.6012	46.37%	641.3117
7	Alabama	Birmingham	88.56%	969.6851	963.0066	6.6785	47.47%	636.5385
8	Oklahoma	Oklahoma City	81.24%	675.4735	664.2818	11.1917	49.18%	551.0374
9	South Carolina	Columbia	94.36%	1470.5946	1467.6462	2.9484	49.53%	734.5777
10	Colorado	Denver	77.83%	734.7589	722.7543	12.0046	49.61%	607.8427
11	Georgia	Atlanta	75.84%	1411.9399	1403.6294	8.3105	51.45%	1018.1935
12	Missouri	Kansas City	68.63%	408.4852	394.7811	13.7041	51.93%	354.5459
13	Kansas	Wichita	83.47%	936.2305	927.2679	8.9626	54.70%	752.272
14	Illinois	Chicago	66.25%	599.0443	588.5273	10.5170	55.06%	563.5726
15	Massachusetts	Boston	76.94%	909.7003	901.9352	7.7651	56.40%	777.6326
16	California	Los Angeles	79.35%	741.8627	732.6973	9.1654	56.65%	668.0541
17	New Jersey	Newark	81.29%	1105.8306	1099.5491	6.2815	57.67%	824.4529
18	New York	New York	81.29%	1105.8306	1099.5491	6.2815	57.67%	824.4529
19	Kentucky	Lexington	93.43%	781.4255	776.9679	4.4576	58.74%	776.9679
20	Minnesota	Minneapolis	70.19%	1565.8816	1555.3019	10.5797	61.09%	1507.6311
21	Florida	Jacksonville	90.76%	1929.4173	1924.8795	4.5378	61.75%	1275.3315
22	Montana	Billings	99.81%	1613.6276	1613.5915	0.0361	63.38%	1352.974
23	Virginia	Virginia Beach	94.98%	1220.2079	1217.7774	2.4305	64.07%	739.7031
24	Michigan	Detroit	88.39%	1426.9336	1421.4859	5.4477	64.47%	900.3915
25	West Virginia	Charleston	96.79%	1272.4727	1270.6955	1.7772	64.99%	1063.4879

Table 12:

Legend: Ranked by Market Share of Banks w/ RvB Calculators (lowest to highest) (Part Two)

	State	MSA	Market Share of Institutions Reviewed	Actual HHI Entire MSA	Actual HH Index Banks Reviewed 1%ers	HHI Point Difference MSA v 1%ers	Market Share of Institutions w/ RvB	Actual HHI RvB Calculators
26	New Mexico	Albuquerque	95.78%	1659.5141	1656.6846	2.8295	66.37%	1327.1815
27	Iowa	Des Moines	85.60%	759.3428	749.9186	9.4242	68.48%	652.5998
28	North Dakota	Fargo	94.59%	1571.9141	1568.5483	3.3658	69.27%	1461.2681
29	Connecticut	Bridgeport	95.10%	1109.3498	1106.2928	3.0570	69.41%	832.9339
30	Idaho	Boise	97.28%	1240.9446	1238.93	2.0146	69.80%	1109.9522
31	Texas	Houston	81.83%	1159.5376	1151.3547	8.1829	71.03%	1133.8195
32	Arkansas	Little Rock	93.30%	786.8591	782.1736	4.6855	71.75%	714.7287
33	Maine	Portland	96.23%	1309.0473	1306.4065	2.6408	72.55%	1222.7809
34	Wyoming	Cheyenne	99.82%	1213.6203	1213.5914	0.0289	72.58%	1093.731
35	Alaska	Anchorage	99.99%	2875.8136	2875.4431	0.3705	72.92%	2209.6602
36	Mississippi	Jackson	95.65%	1971.004	1968.5299	2.4741	74.02%	1865.7394
37	Nebraska	Omaha	84.83%	1335.2406	1328.6897	6.5509	75.31%	1307.9029
38	Washington	Seattle	86.35%	1329.9153	1323.7352	6.1801	75.40%	1295.6341
39	Wisconsin	Milwaukee	84.75%	1365.7213	1357.2607	8.4606	75.72%	1341.6036
40	Indiana	Indianapolis	88.34%	1123.658	1116.92	6.7380	76.80%	1068.2162
41	Louisiana	New Orleans	92.64%	1539.3939	1535.9908	3.4031	79.09%	1513.2575
42	Arizona	Phoenix	89.12%	1509.8192	1505.701	4.1182	80.45%	1480.2103
43	Tennessee	Memphis	86.25%	2959.9872	2953.0785	6.9087	81.23%	2938.1021
44	Rhode Island	Providence	93.97%	1613.9869	1611.3269	2.6600	81.95%	1584.6627
45	Oregon	Portland	91.03%	1330.7678	1325.7025	5.0653	83.16%	1308.652
46	Nevada	Las Vegas	92.24%	4770.0908	4765.2452	4.8456	83.89%	4721.7727
47	Ohio	Columbus	90.37%	1490.3248	1485.8463	4.4785	85.06%	1478.4278
48	New Hampshire	Manchester	97.96%	3023.7918	3022.9252	0.8666	87.98%	2986.983
49	South Dakota	Sioux Falls	94.09%	8145.2937	8142.4683	2.8254	90.19%	8134.2361
50	Hawaii	Honolulu	98.73%	2411.9706	2411.9705	0.0001	97.00%	2408.9776

Table 13:

Legend: Ranked by Actual HHI for Banks w/ RvB Calculators (lowest to highest) (Part One)

	State	MSA	Market Share of Institutions Reviewed	Actual HHI Entire MSA	Actual HH Index Banks Reviewed 1%ers	HHI Point Difference MSA v 1%ers	Market Share of Institutions w/ RvB	Actual HHI RvB Calculators
1	Utah	Salt Lake City	92.71%	2187.3316	2184.1679	3.1637	10.19%	36.2733
2	Pennsylvania	Philadelphia	80.97%	786.3196	779.2625	7.0571	43.90%	319.3636
3	Missouri	Kansas City	68.63%	408.4852	394.7811	13.7041	51.93%	354.5459
4	Oklahoma	Oklahoma City	81.24%	675.4735	664.2818	11.1917	49.18%	551.0374
5	North Carolina	Charlotte	94.87%	4625.7012	4623.1877	2.5135	31.06%	551.4716
6	Illinois	Chicago	66.25%	599.0443	588.5273	10.5170	55.06%	563.5726
7	Colorado	Denver	77.83%	734.7589	722.7543	12.0046	49.61%	607.8427
8	Delaware	Wilmington	95.69%	1741.9743	1740.2407	1.7336	39.82%	632.2762
9	Alabama	Birmingham	88.56%	969.6851	963.0066	6.6785	47.47%	636.5385
10	Vermont	Burlington	99.30%	2332.7978	2332.1966	0.6012	46.37%	641.3117
11	Maryland	Baltimore	81.33%	934.2498	924.8045	9.4453	41.73%	647.6083
12	Iowa	Des Moines	85.60%	759.3428	749.9186	9.4242	68.48%	652.5998
13	California	Los Angeles	79.35%	741.8627	732.6973	9.1654	56.65%	668.0541
14	Arkansas	Little Rock	93.30%	786.8591	782.1736	4.6855	71.75%	714.7287
15	South Carolina	Columbia	94.36%	1470.5946	1467.6462	2.9484	49.53%	734.5777
16	Virginia	Virginia Beach	94.98%	1220.2079	1217.7774	2.4305	64.07%	739.7031
17	Kansas	Wichita	83.47%	936.2305	927.2679	8.9626	54.70%	752.272
18	Kentucky	Lexington	93.43%	781.4255	776.9679	4.4576	58.74%	776.9679
19	Massachusetts	Boston	76.94%	909.7003	901.9352	7.7651	56.40%	777.6326
20	New Jersey	Newark	81.29%	1105.8306	1099.5491	6.2815	57.67%	824.4529
21	New York	New York	81.29%	1105.8306	1099.5491	6.2815	57.67%	824.4529
22	Connecticut	Bridgeport	95.10%	1109.3498	1106.2928	3.0570	69.41%	832.9339
23	Michigan	Detroit	88.39%	1426.9336	1421.4859	5.4477	64.47%	900.3915
24	Georgia	Atlanta	75.84%	1411.9399	1403.6294	8.3105	51.45%	1018.1935
25	West Virginia	Charleston	96.79%	1272.4727	1270.6955	1.7772	64.99%	1063.4879

Table 14:

Legend: Ranked by Actual HHI for Banks w/ RvB Calculators (lowest to highest) (Part Two)

	State	MSA	Market Share of Institutions Reviewed	Actual HHI Entire MSA	Actual HH Index Banks Reviewed 1%ers	HHI Point Difference MSA v 1%ers	Market Share of Institutions w/ RvB	Actual HHI RvB Calculators
26	Indiana	Indianapolis	88.34%	1123.658	1116.92	6.7380	76.80%	1068.2162
27	Wyoming	Cheyenne	99.82%	1213.6203	1213.5914	0.0289	72.58%	1093.731
28	Idaho	Boise	97.28%	1240.9446	1238.93	2.0146	69.80%	1109.9522
29	Texas	Houston	81.83%	1159.5376	1151.3547	8.1829	71.03%	1133.8195
30	Maine	Portland	96.23%	1309.0473	1306.4065	2.6408	72.55%	1222.7809
31	Florida	Jacksonville	90.76%	1929.4173	1924.8795	4.5378	61.75%	1275.3315
32	Washington	Seattle	86.35%	1329.9153	1323.7352	6.1801	75.40%	1295.6341
33	Nebraska	Omaha	84.83%	1335.2406	1328.6897	6.5509	75.31%	1307.9029
34	Oregon	Portland	91.03%	1330.7678	1325.7025	5.0653	83.16%	1308.652
35	New Mexico	Albuquerque	95.78%	1659.5141	1656.6846	2.8295	66.37%	1327.1815
36	Wisconsin	Milwaukee	84.75%	1365.7213	1357.2607	8.4606	75.72%	1341.6036
37	Montana	Billings	99.81%	1613.6276	1613.5915	0.0361	63.38%	1352.974
38	North Dakota	Fargo	94.59%	1571.9141	1568.5483	3.3658	69.27%	1461.2681
39	Ohio	Columbus	90.37%	1490.3248	1485.8463	4.4785	85.06%	1478.4278
40	Arizona	Phoenix	89.12%	1509.8192	1505.701	4.1182	80.45%	1480.2103
41	Minnesota	Minneapolis	70.19%	1565.8816	1555.3019	10.5797	61.09%	1507.6311
42	Louisiana	New Orleans	92.64%	1539.3939	1535.9908	3.4031	79.09%	1513.2575
43	Rhode Island	Providence	93.97%	1613.9869	1611.3269	2.6600	81.95%	1584.6627
44	Mississippi	Jackson	95.65%	1971.004	1968.5299	2.4741	74.02%	1865.7394
45	Alaska	Anchorage	99.99%	2875.8136	2875.4431	0.3705	72.92%	2209.6602
46	Hawaii	Honolulu	98.73%	2411.9706	2411.9705	0.0001	97.00%	2408.9776
47	Tennessee	Memphis	86.25%	2959.9872	2953.0785	6.9087	81.23%	2938.1021
48	New Hampshire	Manchester	97.96%	3023.7918	3022.9252	0.8666	87.98%	2986.983
49	Nevada	Las Vegas	92.24%	4770.0908	4765.2452	4.8456	83.89%	4721.7727
50	South Dakota	Sioux Falls	94.09%	8145.2937	8142.4683	2.8254	90.19%	8134.2361

Table 15:

Legend: Ranked by Pro-Forma HHI for Banks w/ RvB Calculators (lowest to highest) (Part One)

	State	MSA	Market Share of Institutions Reviewed	Actual HHI Institutions Reviewed 1%ers	Actual HHI RvB Calculators	Pro-Forma HHI RvB Calculators	Pro-Forma RvB HHI Point Change	Pro-Forma HH Index MSA
1	Utah	Salt Lake City	92.71%	2184.1679	36.2733	103.8361	67.5628	2254.8862
2	North Carolina	Charlotte	94.87%	4623.1877	551.4716	964.7236	413.2520	5038.8969
3	Delaware	Wilmington	95.69%	1740.2407	632.2762	1585.6324	953.3562	2695.3203
4	Maryland	Baltimore	81.33%	924.8045	647.6083	1741.3929	1093.7846	2027.8939
5	Pennsylvania	Philadelphia	80.97%	779.2625	319.3636	1927.21	1607.8464	2393.6522
6	Vermont	Burlington	99.30%	2332.1966	641.3117	2150.1769	1508.8652	3841.7807
7	Alabama	Birmingham	88.56%	963.0066	636.5385	2253.4009	1616.8624	2586.046
8	Oklahoma	Oklahoma City	81.24%	664.2818	551.0374	2418.6724	1867.6350	2542.6582
9	South Carolina	Columbia	94.36%	1467.6462	734.5777	2453.2209	1718.6432	3189.926
10	Colorado	Denver	77.83%	722.7543	607.8427	2461.1521	1853.3094	3318.4899
11	Georgia	Atlanta	75.84%	1403.6294	1018.1935	2647.1025	1628.9090	3040.9748
12	Missouri	Kansas City	68.63%	394.7811	354.5459	2696.7249	2342.1790	2718.9531
13	Kansas	Wichita	83.47%	927.2679	752.272	2992.09	2239.8180	3175.5565
14	Illinois	Chicago	66.25%	588.5273	563.5726	3031.6036	2468.0310	3065.2984
15	Massachusetts	Boston	76.94%	901.9352	777.6326	3180.96	2403.3274	3313.0241
16	California	Los Angeles	79.35%	732.6973	668.0541	3209.2225	2541.1684	3283.8785
17	New Jersey	Newark	81.29%	1099.5491	824.4529	3325.8289	2501.3760	3606.2026
18	New York	New York	81.29%	1099.5491	824.4529	3325.8289	2501.3760	3606.2026
19	Kentucky	Lexington	93.43%	776.9679	776.9679	3450.3876	2673.4197	3691.7228
20	Minnesota	Minneapolis	70.19%	1555.3019	1507.6311	3731.9881	2224.3570	4130.3483
21	Florida	Jacksonville	90.76%	1924.8795	1275.3315	3813.0625	2537.7310	4468.2371
22	Montana	Billings	99.81%	1613.5915	1352.974	4017.0244	2664.0504	4277.678
23	Virginia	Virginia Beach	94.98%	1217.7774	739.7031	4104.9649	3365.2618	4586.0032
24	Michigan	Detroit	88.39%	1421.4859	900.3915	4156.3809	3255.9894	4648.3077
25	West Virginia	Charleston	96.79%	1270.6955	1063.4879	4223.7001	3160.2122	4430.8412

Table 16:

Legend: Ranked by Pro-Forma HHI for Banks w/ RvB Calculators (lowest to highest) (Part Two)

	State	MSA	Market Share of Institutions Reviewed	Actual HHI Institutions Reviewed 1%ers	Actual HHI RvB Calculators	Pro-Forma HHI RvB Calculators	Pro-Forma RvB HHI Point Change	Pro-Forma HH Index MSA
26	New Mexico	Albuquerque	95.78%	1656.6846	1327.1815	4404.9769	3077.7954	4738.3304
27	Iowa	Des Moines	85.60%	749.9186	652.5998	4689.5104	4036.9106	4794.692
28	North Dakota	Fargo	94.59%	1568.5483	1461.2681	4798.3329	3337.0648	4908.3524
29	Connecticut	Bridgeport	95.10%	1106.2928	832.9339	4817.7481	3984.8142	5095.1143
30	Idaho	Boise	97.28%	1238.93	1109.9522	4872.0400	3762.0878	5004.8252
31	Texas	Houston	81.83%	1151.3547	1133.8195	5045.2609	3911.4414	5071.1348
32	Arkansas	Little Rock	93.30%	782.1736	714.7287	5148.0625	4433.3338	5218.3367
33	Maine	Portland	96.23%	1306.4065	1222.7809	5263.5025	4040.7216	5350.4532
34	Wyoming	Cheyenne	99.82%	1213.5914	1093.731	5267.8564	4174.1254	5387.7457
35	Alaska	Anchorage	99.99%	2875.4431	2209.6602	5317.3264	3107.6662	5983.8658
36	Mississippi	Jackson	95.65%	1968.5299	1865.7394	5478.9604	3613.2210	5584.1833
37	Nebraska	Omaha	84.83%	1328.6897	1307.9029	5671.5961	4363.6932	5698.8956
38	Washington	Seattle	86.35%	1323.7352	1295.6341	5685.16	4389.5259	5718.9491
39	Wisconsin	Milwaukee	84.75%	1357.2607	1341.6036	5733.5184	4391.9148	5758.2123
40	Indiana	Indianapolis	88.34%	1116.92	1068.2162	5898.24	4830.0238	5957.2603
41	Louisiana	New Orleans	92.64%	1535.9908	1513.2575	6255.2281	4741.9706	6281.0394
42	Arizona	Phoenix	89.12%	1505.701	1480.2103	6472.2025	4991.9922	6501.2434
43	Tennessee	Memphis	86.25%	2953.0785	2938.1021	6598.3129	3660.2108	6620.198
44	Rhode Island	Providence	93.97%	1611.3269	1584.6627	6715.8025	5131.1398	6745.124
45	Oregon	Portland	91.03%	1325.7025	1308.652	6915.5856	5606.9336	6937.5638
46	Nevada	Las Vegas	92.24%	4765.2452	4721.7727	7037.5321	2315.7594	7086.3036
47	Ohio	Columbus	90.37%	1485.8463	1478.4278	7235.2036	5756.7758	7248.9356
48	New Hampshire	Manchester	97.96%	3022.9252	2986.983	7740.4804	4753.4974	7777.2975
49	South Dakota	Sioux Falls	94.09%	8142.4683	8134.2361	8134.2361	0.0000	8145.2937
50	Hawaii	Honolulu	98.73%	2411.9705	2408.9776	9409.0000	7000.0224	9412.7572

Table 17:

Legend: Ranked by Pro-Forma HHI Point Change for Banks w/ RvB Calculators (lowest to highest)

	State	MSA	Market Share of Institutions Reviewed	Actual HHI Institutions Reviewed	Actual HHI RvB Calculators	Pro-Forma HHI RvB Calculators	Pro-Forma RvB HHI Point Change	Pro-Forma HH Index MSA
1	South Dakota	Sioux Falls	94.09%	8142.4683	8134.2361	8134.2361	0.0000	8145.2937
2	Utah	Salt Lake City	92.71%	2184.1679	36.2733	103.8361	67.5628	2254.8862
3	North Carolina	Charlotte	94.87%	4623.1877	551.4716	964.7236	413.2520	5038.8969
4	Delaware	Wilmington	95.69%	1740.2407	632.2762	1585.6324	953.3562	2695.3203
5	Maryland	Baltimore	81.33%	924.8045	647.6083	1741.3929	1093.7846	2027.8939
6	Vermont	Burlington	99.30%	2332.1966	641.3117	2150.1769	1508.8652	3841.7807
7	Pennsylvania	Philadelphia	80.97%	779.2625	319.3636	1927.21	1607.8464	2393.6522
8	Alabama	Birmingham	88.56%	963.0066	636.5385	2253.4009	1616.8624	2586.046
9	Georgia	Atlanta	75.84%	1403.6294	1018.1935	2647.1025	1628.9090	3040.9748
10	South Carolina	Columbia	94.36%	1467.6462	734.5777	2453.2209	1718.6432	3189.926
11	Colorado	Denver	77.83%	722.7543	607.8427	2461.1521	1853.3094	3318.4899
12	Oklahoma	Oklahoma City	81.24%	664.2818	551.0374	2418.6724	1867.6350	2542.6582
13	Minnesota	Minneapolis	70.19%	1555.3019	1507.6311	3731.9881	2224.3570	4130.3483
14	Kansas	Wichita	83.47%	927.2679	752.272	2992.09	2239.8180	3175.5565
15	Nevada	Las Vegas	92.24%	4765.2452	4721.7727	7037.5321	2315.7594	7086.3036
16	Missouri	Kansas City	68.63%	394.7811	354.5459	2696.7249	2342.1790	2718.9531
17	Massachusetts	Boston	76.94%	901.9352	777.6326	3180.96	2403.3274	3313.0241
18	Illinois	Chicago	66.25%	588.5273	563.5726	3031.6036	2468.0310	3065.2984
19	New Jersey	Newark	81.29%	1099.5491	824.4529	3325.8289	2501.3760	3606.2026
20	New York	New York	81.29%	1099.5491	824.4529	3325.8289	2501.3760	3606.2026
21	Florida	Jacksonville	90.76%	1924.8795	1275.3315	3813.0625	2537.7310	4468.2371
22	California	Los Angeles	79.35%	732.6973	668.0541	3209.2225	2541.1684	3283.8785
23	Montana	Billings	99.81%	1613.5915	1352.974	4017.0244	2664.0504	4277.678
24	Kentucky	Lexington	93.43%	776.9679	776.9679	3450.3876	2673.4197	3691.7228
25	New Mexico	Albuquerque	95.78%	1656.6846	1327.1815	4404.9769	3077.7954	4738.3304

Table 18:

Legend: Ranked by Pro-Forma HHI Point Change for Banks w/ RvB Calculators (lowest to highest)

	State	MSA	Market Share of Institutions Reviewed	Actual HHI Institutions Reviewed	Actual HHI RvB Calculators	Pro-Forma HHI RvB Calculators	Pro-Forma RvB HHI Point Change	Pro-Forma HH Index MSA
26	Alaska	Anchorage	99.99%	2875.4431	2209.6602	5317.3264	3107.6662	5983.8658
27	West Virginia	Charleston	96.79%	1270.6955	1063.4879	4223.7001	3160.2122	4430.8412
28	Michigan	Detroit	88.39%	1421.4859	900.3915	4156.3809	3255.9894	4648.3077
29	North Dakota	Fargo	94.59%	1568.5483	1461.2681	4798.3329	3337.0648	4908.3524
30	Virginia	Virginia Beach	94.98%	1217.7774	739.7031	4104.9649	3365.2618	4586.0032
31	Mississippi	Jackson	95.65%	1968.5299	1865.7394	5478.9604	3613.2210	5584.1833
32	Tennessee	Memphis	86.25%	2953.0785	2938.1021	6598.3129	3660.2108	6620.198
33	Idaho	Boise	97.28%	1238.93	1109.9522	4872.0400	3762.0878	5004.8252
34	Texas	Houston	81.83%	1151.3547	1133.8195	5045.2609	3911.4414	5071.1348
35	Connecticut	Bridgeport	95.10%	1106.2928	832.9339	4817.7481	3984.8142	5095.1143
36	Iowa	Des Moines	85.60%	749.9186	652.5998	4689.5104	4036.9106	4794.692
37	Maine	Portland	96.23%	1306.4065	1222.7809	5263.5025	4040.7216	5350.4532
38	Wyoming	Cheyenne	99.82%	1213.5914	1093.731	5267.8564	4174.1254	5387.7457
39	Nebraska	Omaha	84.83%	1328.6897	1307.9029	5671.5961	4363.6932	5698.8956
40	Washington	Seattle	86.35%	1323.7352	1295.6341	5685.16	4389.5259	5718.9491
41	Wisconsin	Milwaukee	84.75%	1357.2607	1341.6036	5733.5184	4391.9148	5758.2123
42	Arkansas	Little Rock	93.30%	782.1736	714.7287	5148.0625	4433.3338	5218.3367
43	Louisiana	New Orleans	92.64%	1535.9908	1513.2575	6255.2281	4741.9706	6281.0394
44	New Hampshire	Manchester	97.96%	3022.9252	2986.983	7740.4804	4753.4974	7777.2975
45	Indiana	Indianapolis	88.34%	1116.92	1068.2162	5898.24	4830.0238	5957.2603
46	Arizona	Phoenix	89.12%	1505.701	1480.2103	6472.2025	4991.9922	6501.2434
47	Rhode Island	Providence	93.97%	1611.3269	1584.6627	6715.8025	5131.1398	6745.124
48	Oregon	Portland	91.03%	1325.7025	1308.652	6915.5856	5606.9336	6937.5638
49	Ohio	Columbus	90.37%	1485.8463	1478.4278	7235.2036	5756.7758	7248.9356
50	Hawaii	Honolulu	98.73%	2411.9705	2408.9776	9409.0000	7000.0224	9412.7572

Table 19:

Legend: Ranked by Pro-Forma HHI for MSA (lowest to highest)

	State	MSA	Market Share of Institutions Reviewed	Actual HHI Institutions Reviewed	Actual HHI RvB Calculators	Pro-Forma HHI RvB Calculators	Pro-Forma RvB HHI Point Change	Pro-Forma HH Index MSA
1	Maryland	Baltimore	81.33%	924.8045	647.6083	1741.3929	1093.7846	2027.8939
2	Utah	Salt Lake City	92.71%	2184.1679	36.2733	103.8361	67.5628	2254.8862
3	Pennsylvania	Philadelphia	80.97%	779.2625	319.3636	1927.21	1607.8464	2393.6522
4	Oklahoma	Oklahoma City	81.24%	664.2818	551.0374	2418.6724	1867.6350	2542.6582
5	Alabama	Birmingham	88.56%	963.0066	636.5385	2253.4009	1616.8624	2586.046
6	Delaware	Wilmington	95.69%	1740.2407	632.2762	1585.6324	953.3562	2695.3203
7	Missouri	Kansas City	68.63%	394.7811	354.5459	2696.7249	2342.1790	2718.9531
8	Georgia	Atlanta	75.84%	1403.6294	1018.1935	2647.1025	1628.9090	3040.9748
9	Illinois	Chicago	66.25%	588.5273	563.5726	3031.6036	2468.0310	3065.2984
10	Kansas	Wichita	83.47%	927.2679	752.272	2992.09	2239.8180	3175.5565
11	South Carolina	Columbia	94.36%	1467.6462	734.5777	2453.2209	1718.6432	3189.926
12	California	Los Angeles	79.35%	732.6973	668.0541	3209.2225	2541.1684	3283.8785
13	Massachusetts	Boston	76.94%	901.9352	777.6326	3180.96	2403.3274	3313.0241
14	Colorado	Denver	77.83%	722.7543	607.8427	2461.1521	1853.3094	3318.4899
15	New Jersey	Newark	81.29%	1099.5491	824.4529	3325.8289	2501.3760	3606.2026
16	New York	New York	81.29%	1099.5491	824.4529	3325.8289	2501.3760	3606.2026
17	Kentucky	Lexington	93.43%	776.9679	776.9679	3450.3876	2673.4197	3691.7228
18	Vermont	Burlington	99.30%	2332.1966	641.3117	2150.1769	1508.8652	3841.7807
19	Minnesota	Minneapolis	70.19%	1555.3019	1507.6311	3731.9881	2224.3570	4130.3483
20	Montana	Billings	99.81%	1613.5915	1352.974	4017.0244	2664.0504	4277.678
21	West Virginia	Charleston	96.79%	1270.6955	1063.4879	4223.7001	3160.2122	4430.8412
22	Florida	Jacksonville	90.76%	1924.8795	1275.3315	3813.0625	2537.7310	4468.2371
23	Virginia	Virginia Beach	94.98%	1217.7774	739.7031	4104.9649	3365.2618	4586.0032
24	Michigan	Detroit	88.39%	1421.4859	900.3915	4156.3809	3255.9894	4648.3077
25	New Mexico	Albuquerque	95.78%	1656.6846	1327.1815	4404.9769	3077.7954	4738.3304

Table 20:

Legend: Ranked by Pro-Forma HHI for MSA (lowest to highest)

	State	MSA	Market Share of Institutions Reviewed	Actual HHI Institutions Reviewed	Actual HHI RvB Calculators	Pro-Forma HHI RvB Calculators	Pro-Forma RvB HHI Point Change	Pro-Forma HH Index MSA
26	Iowa	Des Moines	85.60%	749.9186	652.5998	4689.5104	4036.9106	4794.692
27	North Dakota	Fargo	94.59%	1568.5483	1461.2681	4798.3329	3337.0648	4908.3524
28	Idaho	Boise	97.28%	1238.93	1109.9522	4872.0400	3762.0878	5004.8252
29	North Carolina	Charlotte	94.87%	4623.1877	551.4716	964.7236	413.2520	5038.8969
30	Texas	Houston	81.83%	1151.3547	1133.8195	5045.2609	3911.4414	5071.1348
31	Connecticut	Bridgeport	95.10%	1106.2928	832.9339	4817.7481	3984.8142	5095.1143
32	Arkansas	Little Rock	93.30%	782.1736	714.7287	5148.0625	4433.3338	5218.3367
33	Maine	Portland	96.23%	1306.4065	1222.7809	5263.5025	4040.7216	5350.4532
34	Wyoming	Cheyenne	99.82%	1213.5914	1093.731	5267.8564	4174.1254	5387.7457
35	Mississippi	Jackson	95.65%	1968.5299	1865.7394	5478.9604	3613.2210	5584.1833
36	Nebraska	Omaha	84.83%	1328.6897	1307.9029	5671.5961	4363.6932	5698.8956
37	Washington	Seattle	86.35%	1323.7352	1295.6341	5685.16	4389.5259	5718.9491
38	Wisconsin	Milwaukee	84.75%	1357.2607	1341.6036	5733.5184	4391.9148	5758.2123
39	Indiana	Indianapolis	88.34%	1116.92	1068.2162	5898.24	4830.0238	5957.2603
40	Alaska	Anchorage	99.99%	2875.4431	2209.6602	5317.3264	3107.6662	5983.8658
41	Louisiana	New Orleans	92.64%	1535.9908	1513.2575	6255.2281	4741.9706	6281.0394
42	Arizona	Phoenix	89.12%	1505.701	1480.2103	6472.2025	4991.9922	6501.2434
43	Tennessee	Memphis	86.25%	2953.0785	2938.1021	6598.3129	3660.2108	6620.198
44	Rhode Island	Providence	93.97%	1611.3269	1584.6627	6715.8025	5131.1398	6745.124
45	Oregon	Portland	91.03%	1325.7025	1308.652	6915.5856	5606.9336	6937.5638
46	Nevada	Las Vegas	92.24%	4765.2452	4721.7727	7037.5321	2315.7594	7086.3036
47	Ohio	Columbus	90.37%	1485.8463	1478.4278	7235.2036	5756.7758	7248.9356
48	New Hampshire	Manchester	97.96%	3022.9252	2986.983	7740.4804	4753.4974	7777.2975
49	South Dakota	Sioux Falls	94.09%	8142.4683	8134.2361	8134.2361	0.0000	8145.2937
50	Hawaii	Honolulu	98.73%	2411.9705	2408.9776	9409.0000	7000.0224	9412.7572

Table 21:

Legend: Ranked by Number of Banking Institutions in the MSA (lowest to highest)

	State	MSA	Number of Institutions In MSA	Market Share of Institutions Reviewed	# Institutions Reviewed	Market Share of Institutions w/ RvB	# Institutions With RvB Calculators	Pro-Forma # Institutions In MSA
1	Alaska	Anchorage	5	99.99%	5	72.92%	3	3
2	Vermont	Burlington	9	99.30%	7	46.37%	4	6
3	Hawaii	Honolulu	12	98.73%	7	97.00%	6	7
4	Montana	Billings	13	99.81%	12	63.38%	4	10
5	New Hampshire	Manchester	13	97.96%	7	87.98%	4	10
6	Wyoming	Cheyenne	17	99.82%	15	72.58%	6	13
7	Idaho	Boise	21	97.28%	16	69.80%	9	13
8	New Mexico	Albuquerque	22	95.78%	9	66.37%	5	18
9	Maine	Portland	23	96.23%	15	72.55%	7	17
10	Mississippi	Jackson	23	95.65%	13	74.02%	5	19
11	West Virginia	Charleston	23	96.79%	15	64.99%	7	17
12	South Carolina	Columbia	24	94.36%	10	49.53%	4	21
13	North Dakota	Fargo	25	94.59%	15	69.27%	7	19
14	Connecticut	Bridgeport	30	95.10%	16	69.41%	11	20
15	South Dakota	Sioux Falls	33	94.09%	3	90.19%	1	33
16	Virginia	Virginia Beach	33	94.98%	15	64.07%	9	25
17	Kentucky	Lexington	35	93.43%	22	58.74%	10	26
18	Arkansas	Little Rock	37	93.30%	23	71.75%	14	24
19	Florida	Jacksonville	38	90.76%	12	61.75%	8	31
20	Rhode Island	Providence	40	93.97%	15	81.95%	9	32
21	Nevada	Las Vegas	41	92.24%	7	83.89%	5	37
22	Louisiana	New Orleans	42	92.64%	17	79.09%	8	35
23	Oregon	Portland	42	91.03%	12	83.16%	8	35
24	Delaware	Wilmington	43	95.69%	11	39.82%	3	41
25	Alabama	Birmingham	44	88.56%	14	47.47%	4	41

Table 22:

Legend: Ranked by Number of Banking Institutions in the MSA (lowest to highest)

	State	MSA	Number of Institutions In MSA	Market Share of Institutions Reviewed	# Institutions Reviewed 1%ers	Market Share of Institutions w/ RvB	# Institutions With RvB Calculators	Pro-Forma # Institutions In MSA
26	North Carolina	Charlotte	46	94.87%	6	31.06%	5	42
27	Iowa	Des Moines	53	85.60%	18	68.48%	12	42
28	Indiana	Indianapolis	56	88.34%	16	76.80%	12	45
29	Tennessee	Memphis	56	86.25%	11	81.23%	9	48
30	Kansas	Wichita	59	83.47%	15	54.70%	7	53
31	Michigan	Detroit	61	88.39%	9	64.47%	7	55
32	Ohio	Columbus	61	90.37%	14	85.06%	10	52
33	Utah	Salt Lake City	61	92.71%	14	10.19%	3	59
34	Wisconsin	Milwaukee	65	84.75%	17	75.72%	11	55
35	Arizona	Phoenix	67	89.12%	12	80.45%	9	59
36	Oklahoma	Oklahoma City	67	81.24%	20	49.18%	8	60
37	Nebraska	Omaha	74	84.83%	14	75.31%	9	66
38	Washington	Seattle	76	86.35%	13	75.40%	8	69
39	Colorado	Denver	86	77.83%	17	49.61%	7	79
40	Maryland	Baltimore	90	81.33%	17	41.73%	6	85
41	Texas	Houston	110	81.83%	17	71.03%	10	101
42	Georgia	Atlanta	152	75.84%	11	51.45%	7	146
43	Missouri	Kansas City	156	68.63%	20	51.93%	11	146
44	Massachusetts	Boston	157	76.94%	14	56.40%	9	149
45	Pennsylvania	Philadelphia	158	80.97%	12	43.90%	8	151
46	California	Los Angeles	164	79.35%	17	56.65%	8	157
47	Minnesota	Minneapolis	183	70.19%	7	61.09%	5	178
48	New Jersey	Newark	242	81.29%	17	57.67%	12	231
49	New York	New York	242	81.29%	17	57.67%	12	231
50	Illinois	Chicago	305	66.25%	16	55.06%	10	296

Table 23:

Legend: Ranked by Number of Banks (1%ers) Reviewed (lowest to highest) (Part One)

	State	MSA	Number of Institutions In MSA	Market Share of Institutions Reviewed	Number of Institutions Reviewed 1%ers	Market Share of Institutions w/ RvB	# Institutions With RvB Calculators	Pro-Forma # Institutions In MSA
1	South Dakota	Sioux Falls	33	94.09%	3	90.19%	1	33
2	Alaska	Anchorage	5	99.99%	5	72.92%	3	3
3	North Carolina	Charlotte	46	94.87%	6	31.06%	5	42
4	Vermont	Burlington	9	99.30%	7	46.37%	4	6
5	Hawaii	Honolulu	12	98.73%	7	97.00%	6	7
6	New Hampshire	Manchester	13	97.96%	7	87.98%	4	10
7	Nevada	Las Vegas	41	92.24%	7	83.89%	5	37
8	Minnesota	Minneapolis	183	70.19%	7	61.09%	5	178
9	New Mexico	Albuquerque	22	95.78%	9	66.37%	5	18
10	Michigan	Detroit	61	88.39%	9	64.47%	7	55
11	South Carolina	Columbia	24	94.36%	10	49.53%	4	21
12	Delaware	Wilmington	43	95.69%	11	39.82%	3	41
13	Tennessee	Memphis	56	86.25%	11	81.23%	9	48
14	Georgia	Atlanta	152	75.84%	11	51.45%	7	146
15	Montana	Billings	13	99.81%	12	63.38%	4	10
16	Florida	Jacksonville	38	90.76%	12	61.75%	8	31
17	Oregon	Portland	42	91.03%	12	83.16%	8	35
18	Arizona	Phoenix	67	89.12%	12	80.45%	9	59
19	Pennsylvania	Philadelphia	158	80.97%	12	43.90%	8	151
20	Mississippi	Jackson	23	95.65%	13	74.02%	5	19
21	Washington	Seattle	76	86.35%	13	75.40%	8	69
22	Alabama	Birmingham	44	88.56%	14	47.47%	4	41
23	Ohio	Columbus	61	90.37%	14	85.06%	10	52
24	Utah	Salt Lake City	61	92.71%	14	10.19%	3	59
25	Nebraska	Omaha	74	84.83%	14	75.31%	9	66

Table 24:

Legend: Ranked by Number of Banking Institutions (1%ers) Reviewed (lowest to highest) (Part Two)

	State	MSA	Number of Institutions In MSA	Market Share of Institutions Reviewed	Number of Institutions Reviewed 1%ers	Market Share of Institutions w/ RvB	# Institutions With RvB Calculators	Pro-Forma # Institutions In MSA
26	Massachusetts	Boston	157	76.94%	14	56.40%	9	149
27	Wyoming	Cheyenne	17	99.82%	15	72.58%	6	13
28	Maine	Portland	23	96.23%	15	72.55%	7	17
29	West Virginia	Charleston	23	96.79%	15	64.99%	7	17
30	North Dakota	Fargo	25	94.59%	15	69.27%	7	19
31	Virginia	Virginia Beach	33	94.98%	15	64.07%	9	25
32	Rhode Island	Providence	40	93.97%	15	81.95%	9	32
33	Kansas	Wichita	59	83.47%	15	54.70%	7	53
34	Idaho	Boise	21	97.28%	16	69.80%	9	13
35	Connecticut	Bridgeport	30	95.10%	16	69.41%	11	20
36	Indiana	Indianapolis	56	88.34%	16	76.80%	12	45
37	Illinois	Chicago	305	66.25%	16	55.06%	10	296
38	Louisiana	New Orleans	42	92.64%	17	79.09%	8	35
39	Wisconsin	Milwaukee	65	84.75%	17	75.72%	11	55
40	Colorado	Denver	86	77.83%	17	49.61%	7	79
41	Maryland	Baltimore	90	81.33%	17	41.73%	6	85
42	Texas	Houston	110	81.83%	17	71.03%	10	101
43	California	Los Angeles	164	79.35%	17	56.65%	8	157
44	New Jersey	Newark	242	81.29%	17	57.67%	12	231
45	New York	New York	242	81.29%	17	57.67%	12	231
46	Iowa	Des Moines	53	85.60%	18	68.48%	12	42
47	Oklahoma	Oklahoma City	67	81.24%	20	49.18%	8	60
48	Missouri	Kansas City	156	68.63%	20	51.93%	11	146
49	Kentucky	Lexington	35	93.43%	22	58.74%	10	26
50	Arkansas	Little Rock	37	93.30%	23	71.75%	14	24

Table 25:

Legend: Ranked by Number of Banks w/ RvB Calculators (1%ers) (lowest to highest) (Part One)

	State	MSA	Number of Institutions In MSA	Market Share of Institutions Reviewed	Number of Institutions Reviewed	Market Share of Institutions w/ RvB	# Institutions With RvB Calculators	Pro-Forma # Institutions In MSA
1	South Dakota	Sioux Falls	33	94.09%	3	90.19%	1	33
2	Alaska	Anchorage	5	99.99%	5	72.92%	3	3
3	Delaware	Wilmington	43	95.69%	11	39.82%	3	41
4	Utah	Salt Lake City	61	92.71%	14	10.19%	3	59
5	Vermont	Burlington	9	99.30%	7	46.37%	4	6
6	New Hampshire	Manchester	13	97.96%	7	87.98%	4	10
7	South Carolina	Columbia	24	94.36%	10	49.53%	4	21
8	Montana	Billings	13	99.81%	12	63.38%	4	10
9	Alabama	Birmingham	44	88.56%	14	47.47%	4	41
10	North Carolina	Charlotte	46	94.87%	6	31.06%	5	42
11	Nevada	Las Vegas	41	92.24%	7	83.89%	5	37
12	Minnesota	Minneapolis	183	70.19%	7	61.09%	5	178
13	New Mexico	Albuquerque	22	95.78%	9	66.37%	5	18
14	Mississippi	Jackson	23	95.65%	13	74.02%	5	19
15	Hawaii	Honolulu	12	98.73%	7	97.00%	6	7
16	Wyoming	Cheyenne	17	99.82%	15	72.58%	6	13
17	Maryland	Baltimore	90	81.33%	17	41.73%	6	85
18	Michigan	Detroit	61	88.39%	9	64.47%	7	55
19	Georgia	Atlanta	152	75.84%	11	51.45%	7	146
20	Maine	Portland	23	96.23%	15	72.55%	7	17
21	West Virginia	Charleston	23	96.79%	15	64.99%	7	17
22	North Dakota	Fargo	25	94.59%	15	69.27%	7	19
23	Kansas	Wichita	59	83.47%	15	54.70%	7	53
24	Colorado	Denver	86	77.83%	17	49.61%	7	79
25	Florida	Jacksonville	38	90.76%	12	61.75%	8	31

Table 26:

Legend: Ranked by Number of Banks w/ RvB Calculators (1%ers) (lowest to highest) (Part Two)

	State	MSA	Number of Institutions In MSA	Market Share of Institutions Reviewed	Number of Institutions Reviewed	Market Share of Institutions w/ RvB	# Institutions With RvB Calculators	Pro-Forma # Institutions In MSA
26	Oregon	Portland	42	91.03%	12	83.16%	8	35
27	Pennsylvania	Philadelphia	158	80.97%	12	43.90%	8	151
28	Washington	Seattle	76	86.35%	13	75.40%	8	69
29	Louisiana	New Orleans	42	92.64%	17	79.09%	8	35
30	California	Los Angeles	164	79.35%	17	56.65%	8	157
31	Oklahoma	Oklahoma City	67	81.24%	20	49.18%	8	60
32	Tennessee	Memphis	56	86.25%	11	81.23%	9	48
33	Arizona	Phoenix	67	89.12%	12	80.45%	9	59
34	Nebraska	Omaha	74	84.83%	14	75.31%	9	66
35	Massachusetts	Boston	157	76.94%	14	56.40%	9	149
36	Virginia	Virginia Beach	33	94.98%	15	64.07%	9	25
37	Rhode Island	Providence	40	93.97%	15	81.95%	9	32
38	Idaho	Boise	21	97.28%	16	69.80%	9	13
39	Ohio	Columbus	61	90.37%	14	85.06%	10	52
40	Illinois	Chicago	305	66.25%	16	55.06%	10	296
41	Texas	Houston	110	81.83%	17	71.03%	10	101
42	Kentucky	Lexington	35	93.43%	22	58.74%	10	26
43	Connecticut	Bridgeport	30	95.10%	16	69.41%	11	20
44	Wisconsin	Milwaukee	65	84.75%	17	75.72%	11	55
45	Missouri	Kansas City	156	68.63%	20	51.93%	11	146
46	Indiana	Indianapolis	56	88.34%	16	76.80%	12	45
47	New Jersey	Newark	242	81.29%	17	57.67%	12	231
48	New York	New York	242	81.29%	17	57.67%	12	231
49	Iowa	Des Moines	53	85.60%	18	68.48%	12	42
50	Arkansas	Little Rock	37	93.30%	23	71.75%	14	24

[i] http://www.huduser.org/publications/pdf/treasrpt.pdf
[ii] http://www.occ.treas.gov/
[iii] http://www.ots.treas.gov/
[iv] http://www.bankofamerica.com/loansandhomes/index.cfm?template=learn_calculators&statecheck=GA
[v] Ibid
[vi] www.mortgage-calc.com
[vii] www.interst.com/contents/calculators/rentvsbuy.asp
[viii] www.bloomberg.com/invest/calculators/rentbuy.html
[ix] http://partners.Leadfusion.com/tools/suntrust/home08/tool.fc
[x] http://www.federalreserve.gov/releases/h15/20061204/
[xi] http://www.irs.gov/irb/2005-46_IRB/ar09.html
[xii] IRS Publication No. 527, page 6 (2006 v.)
[xiii] Ibid
[xiv] http://msucares.com/pubs/publications/p1661.htm
[xv] http://web.mit.edu/cre/research/hai/aff-index.html
[xvi] http://www.hud.gov/buying/index.cfm
[xvii] Note: The Calculator uses these items in its calculations: "private mortgage insurance, homeowner's insurance cost, loan closing costs, cost of selling a home, property tax, homeowner's tax savings, and rent increases. Calculator results are estimates only."
[xviii] http://www.mtgprofessor.com/mpcalculators/AmortizationSchedWithTaxSavings/TaxSavings.asp
[xix] http://www.smartmoney.com/home/buying/index.cfm?story=rentown
[xx] You are informed that before any program is awarded the exclusive ABA Seal of Approval, CAB puts it through an extensive due diligence review, including independent analysis by industry experts and testing and validation by bankers in the field. When a solution bears the ABA seal, you can rely on that solution to provide top quality performance and reliable results. The calculator has a disclaimer that is not endorsed by the ABA.
[xxi] http://www.aba.com/solutions/mortgage_lending.htm
[xxii] Ibid
[xxiii] Ibid
[xxiv] 15 U.S.C § 45.
[xxv] 15 U.S.C § 57.
[xxvi] Financial Institutions Letters, Statement of the Board of Governors of the Federal Reserve System and the Federal Deposit Insurance Corporation, *Unfair or deceptive Acts or Practices by State –Chartered Banks* (March 11, 2004).
[xxvii] Ibid
[xxviii] Ibid
[xxix] Ibid
[xxx] Ibid
[xxxi] Ibid
[xxxii] Ibid
[xxxiii] http://www.huduser.org/publications/pdf/treasrpt.pdf
[xxxiv] Black's Law Dictionary, 7th Edition, page 670
[xxxv] Black's Law Dictionary, 7th Edition, page 476
[xxxvi] Black's Law Dictionary, 7th Edition, page 477
[xxxvii] Example given, HUD, Ginnie Mae, Freddie Mac
[xxxviii] Jack M. Guttentag, Professor of Finance Emeritus at the Wharton School of the University of Pennsylvania

www.ingramcontent.com/pod-product-compliance
Lightning Source LLC
LaVergne TN
LVHW070953210926
848482LV00002B/206
* 9 7 8 0 9 7 6 4 9 6 7 4 8 *